PRAISE FOR THE PLAYS OF RAJIV JOSEPH

GRUESOME PLAYGROUND INJURIES

Gruesome Playground Injuries finds a fresh way of expressing human vulnerability, and two individuals' struggle to understand their need for each other. Joseph takes risks . . . that pay off emotionally."

—EVERETT EVANS, *Houston Chronicle*

"Make[s] us feel life's brevity and fragility . . . there's something paradoxically life-affirming about the sensitivity with which playwright and players perform this haunting ode to self-destruction."

—CHRIS KLIMEK, *Washington City Paper*

"A provocative dark comedy."   —Olivia Florez Alvarez, *Houston Press*

"Layered with quirky humor and poignant intensity—a crash course in growing up, getting hurt, and the healing power of love."

—GWENDOLYN PURDOM, *Washingtonian*

ANIMALS OUT OF PAPER

"Joseph's observant, pitch-perfect script seems modest at first but is really quite ambitious, dealing ruthlessly . . . with the fragility of happiness, the tragedy of impulsiveness and the tenuousness of hope."

—ANITA GATES, *The New York Times*

"Terrific . . . Joseph's carefully modulated play slowly reveals darker edges to these characters."   —JASON CLARK, *Entertainment Weekly*

"[Joseph] begins with a quirky comedy about origami experts and deftly transforms it into a melancholy reminder that close friends make the worst messes. His journey from one extreme to the other . . . is surprising and specific, pulling honest insights out of unusual situations."

—MARK BLANKENSHIP, *Variety*

"Rajiv Joseph is one of the most refreshing new playwrights I've ever encountered . . . *Animals Out of Paper* is one of the most satisfying new works I've seen all year. Joseph is a fascinating voice in the world of theatre. He's crafted a substantial play, funny and sad, down-to-earth and unpretentious, with a great deal of meaning . . . Joseph's play is refreshingly genuine, and he's a playwright to look out for."

—DAVID GORDON, nytheatre.com

BENGAL TIGER AT THE BAGHDAD ZOO

"No ordinary play. I'm tempted to call it the most original drama written so far about the Iraq war, but why sell the work short? The imagination behind it is way too thrillingly genre-busting to be confined within such a limiting category . . . *Bengal Tiger* marks the breakthrough of a major new playwriting talent."

—CHARLES MCNULTY, *Los Angeles Times*

"The writing is beautiful . . . the pacing is taut and thrilling."

—LAURENCE VITTES, *The Hollywood Reporter*

"Quite magnificent."   —STEVEN LEIGH MORRIS, *LA Weekly*

"Though set amid the throes of the U.S. incursion, it's less an Iraq War play than a heavily metaphorical musing on life's purpose in a godless universe."

—BOB VERINI, *Variety*

RAJIV JOSEPH

GRUESOME PLAYGROUND INJURIES
ANIMALS OUT OF PAPER
BENGAL TIGER AT THE BAGHDAD ZOO

RAJIV JOSEPH's plays include *Huck & Holden*, *All This Intimacy*, and *The Leopard and the Fox*. He has been the recipient of a grant for Outstanding New American Play from the National Endowment for the Arts for *Bengal Tiger at the Baghdad Zoo*, which was a Pulitzer Prize finalist for Drama in 2010; a Lucille Lortel Award Nomination for Outstanding Play for *Animals Out of Paper*; the Paula Vogel Award in Playwriting; and a Kesselring Fellowship for emerging dramatists from The National Arts Club.

In 2009 he received the Whiting Writers Award, given annually to ten emerging writers in fiction, nonfiction, poetry, and plays.

He received his BA in creative writing from Miami University and his MFA in playwriting from NYU's Tisch School of the Arts. Born and raised in Cleveland, Ohio, he served for three years in the Peace Corps in Senegal, West Africa, and now makes his home in Brooklyn, New York.

three plays

RAJIV JOSEPH

GRUESOME PLAYGROUND INJURIES
ANIMALS OUT OF PAPER
BENGAL TIGER AT THE BAGHDAD ZOO
GRUESOME PLAYGROUND INJURIES
ANIMALS OUT OF PAPER
BENGAL TIGER AT THE BAGHDAD ZOO
GRUESOME PLAYGROUND INJURIES
ANIMALS OUT OF PAPER
BENGAL TIGER AT THE BAGHDAD ZOO
GRUESOME PLAYGROUND INJURIES
ANIMALS OUT OF PAPER
BENGAL TIGER AT THE BAGHDAD ZOO
GRUESOME PLAYGROUND INJURIES
ANIMALS OUT OF PAPER
BENGAL TIGER AT THE BAGHDAD ZOO

SOFT SKULL PRESS
AN IMPRINT OF
COUNTERPOINT BERKELEY

Library of Congress Cataloging-in-Publication Data

Joseph, Rajiv.
  Gruesome playground injuries ; Animals out of paper ; Bengal tiger at the Baghdad Zoo :
three plays / Rajiv Joseph.
    p. cm.
  Includes bibliographical references and index.
  ISBN 978-1-59376-294-0 (alk. paper)
  I. Joseph, Rajiv. Animals out of paper. II. Joseph, Rajib. Bengal tiger at the Baghdad Zoo. III. Title.
  PS3610.O669G78 2010
  822'.92--dc22

                            2010029075

Cover design by Jason Torchinsky
Interior design by Neuwirth and Associates
Printed in the United States of America

Soft Skull Press
An Imprint of Counterpoint LLC
1919 Fifth Street
Berkeley, CA 94710

www.softskull.com
www.counterpointpress.com

Distributed by Publishers Group West

10 9 8 7 6

THIS BOOK IS FOR MY AUNTS:

Anita Notley
Helenmarie Zachritz
Joanne Joseph
Iona Abraham
Freda Swaminathan
Rosalind Gauchat
and
Colette Gauchat

CONTENTS

GRUESOME PLAYGROUND INJURIES

PRODUCTION HISTORY

Gruesome Playground Injuries had its world premiere on October 16, 2009, at the Alley Theatre in Houston, Texas. Rebecca Taichman, Director; Riccardo Hernandez, Scenic Design; Miranda Hoffman, Costume Designer; Christopher Akerlind, Lighting Design; Jill BC DuBoff, Sound Design; and Mark Bly, Dramaturge.

KAYLEEN: Selma Blair
DOUG: Brad Fleischer

Gruesome Playground Injuries had its Off-Broadway premiere in February 2011 at Second Stage Theater. Scott Ellis, Director; Carole Rothman, Artistic Director; Christopher Burney, Associate Artistic Director.

At the time this edition went to press, the play had not yet been cast.

CHARACTERS

KAYLEEN: ages eight to thirty-eight
DOUG: ages eight to thirty-eight

SETTING

Various places over the course of thirty years

NOTE

All transitions between the scenes should be done by the actors, and their changing of the scene should be leisurely. Costume changes should occur on stage. There is no need to hide any of this work from the audience. We should especially see Doug's dressing of his wounds, or the application of the necessary makeup that represents his injuries. The lengths of the transitions signify and allow for large passages of time in the lives of the characters. Every scene either jumps forward fifteen years, or backward ten years.

At times in the dialogue, there are questions but no question mark is written. Absence of a question mark is purposeful. When there is no question mark, the question is delivered in a flat, non-inquiring tone.

ACT 1
Scene 1. Eight: Face Split Open

> *A nurse's office in an elementary school. Two beds across from one another.*
>
> *Kayleen, eight, lies on one of the beds, not sleeping. She begins to hit the mattress with her hands rhythmically. She stops. She sits up. She stands on the bed, absently. She's bored. She bounces a little on the bed, and then stops.*
>
> *A sound of someone coming from outside. Kayleen drops back down and pretends to sleep.*
>
> *Doug, eight, enters. He has a large gauze bandage wrapped and taped across his face. An awful dark stain of blood grows in the middle of the bandage. He seems dazed, but not hurt, not crying.*
>
> *He sits on the edge of the other bed and stares at Kayleen. She sits up.*

KAYLEEN: What happened to your face?

DOUG: I fell.

KAYLEEN: Why.

DOUG: I don't know.

KAYLEEN: Does it hurt?

DOUG: A little.

KAYLEEN: I have a stomachache. Sometimes food makes me sick. My mom says it's because I have bad thoughts.

DOUG: Like what?

KAYLEEN: Bad thoughts.

DOUG: Like about Dracula?

KAYLEEN: About stomachs.

DOUG: I have bad thoughts about Dracula.

KAYLEEN: Yeah.

DOUG: Blood tastes funny. It tastes like fruit.

KAYLEEN: It does not.

DOUG: Have you ever cut your face open?

KAYLEEN: No.

DOUG: I get cut all the time by accident.

KAYLEEN: I like the nurse's office. It is quiet and dark.

DOUG: I had a stomachache when I went and saw the movies.

KAYLEEN: I like the movies except when I come out and there is sun.

DOUG: I had three big Cokes. And I had gummy worms. I like to swallow them like real worms.

KAYLEEN: Why do you have so much blood?

DOUG: Because I fell.

KAYLEEN: Why'd you fall?

DOUG: I rode my bike off the roof.

KAYLEEN: What roof?

DOUG: This roof.

KAYLEEN: The school roof?

DOUG: Yeah.

KAYLEEN: Why.

DOUG: I was playing Evel Knievel.

KAYLEEN: What's Evel Knievel?

DOUG: He's a motorcycle guy.
That's how I broke my face.

KAYLEEN: Your face isn't broken, it's just cut.

DOUG: Sister Mary Pat said I broke my face.

KAYLEEN: Does it hurt?

DOUG: One time? I went ice skating with my brothers? And I fell on the ice and this girl skated by me and her ice skate cut my eyelid open and I was bleeding out of my eye. I couldn't see because of all the blood.

KAYLEEN: Did it hurt?

DOUG: No, because the eyelid is small even though there is a lot of blood. I have a scar on my eye.
Girls don't get scars.

KAYLEEN: Yes we do.

DOUG: How come?

KAYLEEN: If you rode your bike off the roof, then how did you get the bike on the roof?

DOUG: I climbed up a tree.

KAYLEEN: You took your bike with you up the tree?

DOUG: Yeah.

KAYLEEN: Why.

DOUG: So I could ride it off the roof.

KAYLEEN: And then you rode your bike off the roof?

DOUG: Yeah.

Beat.

KAYLEEN: You're stupid.

DOUG: I am not.

KAYLEEN: Yes you are.

DOUG: Shut up.

KAYLEEN: You shut up.

Long silence.

KAYLEEN: One time, I threw up because I had a stomachache and I threw up so bad that my one eye started to have blood in it.

DOUG: Why.

KAYLEEN: Because I threw up so hard and so there was blood in my eye.

DOUG: Did it hurt?

KAYLEEN: No. But it was red.
   I have a sensitive stomach. The doctor told me.
   There's an angel on the roof.

DOUG: No there's not.

KAYLEEN: Yes there is. It's a statue.
   Are you going to go to the doctor's?

DOUG: To get stitches. I like to get stitches.

KAYLEEN: Why.

DOUG: It makes your skin feel tight.

KAYLEEN: Does it hurt?

DOUG: Yeah.

Kayleen gets up and wanders around the room.

KAYLEEN: This room is like a dungeon.

DOUG: What's a dungeon?

KAYLEEN: It's a room in a castle. It's where people languish.

DOUG: Oh.

KAYLEEN: The rest of the castle is loud and has bright lights and flags and hot oil because of wars. But the dungeon is where people can go to languish and get some peace and quiet.

DOUG: *(sudden; with great pain)* Ow!

KAYLEEN: What?

DOUG: *(normal)* My face hurts. I broke it.

KAYLEEN: You did not. It's just cut.
   Can I see it?

DOUG: What?

KAYLEEN: Can I see the cut on your face?

DOUG: Why.

KAYLEEN: Can I?

> *Doug slowly takes off his gauze bandage to reveal a huge gash.*
>
> *Kayleen looks at it for a long time. Doug looks at Kayleen looking at his wounds.*

KAYLEEN: Does it hurt?

DOUG: A little.

> *Kayleen continues looking at his cut. Doug continues looking at her.*

DOUG: What happened to the blood in your eye?

KAYLEEN: It went back into my head.

> *They continue looking at each other.*

KAYLEEN: Can I touch it?

DOUG: Why.

KAYLEEN: Can I?

DOUG: Okay.

> *Kayleen touches Doug's wound.*

KAYLEEN: Gross.

DOUG: Your hands are cold.

KAYLEEN: It's because I wash them a lot. You should wash your hands. They are grimy.

DOUG: *(showing his hands)* I fell. There's pieces of rock in them.

> *Kayleen kneels down and takes his hand and starts to pick pieces of gravel out of his palm. Doug stares at her, transfixed, as she does this.*

DOUG: *(quietly)* Ow.

KAYLEEN: Does it hurt?

DOUG: A little.

> *Lights shift. Music fills and Kayleen and Doug prepare for scene two.*

Scene 2. Twenty-three: Eye Blown Out

> *Fifteen years later. The kids are twenty-three.*
>
> *A hospital room. Doug sits on an examining table. He's wearing a black suit spattered with blood. He has an enormous bandage across his face, covering specifically his left eye. He looks dazed. His front tooth is missing.*
>
> *Kayleen enters. She wears a black dress and heels. She also looks dazed. She has mud all over her feet and lower legs.*
>
> *She sees Doug like this for the first time.*
>
> *They stare at each other.*

DOUG: Leave me alone.

KAYLEEN: Dougie.

What did you do.

DOUG: The fireworks were awesome. Except for the one that went in my eye.

(re: the mud on her legs; her state) What happened to *you*?

KAYLEEN: I fell asleep at the kitchen table.

DOUG: What?

KAYLEEN: I just did. I had some drinks when I got home.

DOUG: What about that guy. That guy. That guy you live with.

KAYLEEN: He's sleeping. He was sleeping when I got home. His name is Brad.

DOUG: His name is ass-face.

KAYLEEN: Why'd you do this?

DOUG: Why do you have mud all over your legs.

KAYLEEN: Why'd you do this?

DOUG: I asked you first.

KAYLEEN: You *did not.* Stop acting like a child. You're such a spaz. You shouldn't be left alone with explosives.

DOUG: I didn't want to be alone.

KAYLEEN: It's all *my* fault now.

The night before I have to bury my father.

DOUG: What are you even doing here?

KAYLEEN: Kristen MacConnell called me.

DOUG: Kristen from high school?

KAYLEEN: She's a nurse here. She said you came in and you kept saying my name. So she called me.

They thought you tried to kill yourself.

DOUG: Who tries to kill themself with a firework?

KAYLEEN: I know.

I told them, no, you're just a crackhead dumb ass with shit for brains. I told them you'd never commit suicide because you wouldn't have any scars to show off afterward.

Anyway, she said you got hurt.

DOUG: Why'd you come?

KAYLEEN: I don't know, Dougie. I was asleep on the kitchen table and Kristen calls me from the freaking hospital.
Look at you.
Your tooth and now your eye.

DOUG: Why do you have mud all over your legs.

KAYLEEN: I drove halfway, but the car got stuck in the mud.

DOUG: What do you mean?

KAYLEEN: I mean, I drove part of the way until the car got stuck in the mud.

DOUG: The car got stuck in the mud.

KAYLEEN: Yeah.

DOUG: What are you even talking about? What mud? Where is there mud between the hospital and your house that you could get stuck in?

KAYLEEN: Just don't . . . Just shut up.
There's mud.
On the side of the road.

DOUG: What, you veered off the road? Are you drunk?

KAYLEEN: No!
It's just the windshield is all jacked up because Brad hit a tree last February, and I couldn't see, and there was this mist or fog or something.
And I drank a few vodkas. But I mostly slept those off.

DOUG: So you just left the car.

KAYLEEN: You know how I get.

DOUG: How you get?

KAYLEEN: Fuck you. You know how I get.

When you get hurt.
You know.

DOUG: *(matter of fact)* Doctor said I'm gonna be blind in one eye.

KAYLEEN: *(quietly)* Dougie . . .

> *She sits near him, covers her eyes briefly with her hands.*

DOUG: *(not sad, just observing)* It's gone. The whole thing. But I think it wasn't just the poke. It was the burn too. The thing kept burning once it had punctured the eye. And so the burn really messed it all up.

KAYLEEN: You always had problems with that eye.

DOUG: Yeah.

KAYLEEN: The chopping wedge.

DOUG: The wedge.

KAYLEEN: And that girl who skated on your eye, right? When you were little?
And then senior year. The Tabasco sauce.

DOUG: And pinkeye.

KAYLEEN: Yeah.

DOUG: I gave you pinkeye that time.

KAYLEEN: No, you didn't. I never got it.

DOUG: I think about that all the time.
(beat) I think about that all the time. I always think about it.

KAYLEEN: Yeah, well, you're a freak.
I'm fat.

DOUG: I didn't want you to come in here.

KAYLEEN: Yeah, right.

DOUG: I mean, I'm glad you're here. For sure. But you have the funeral tomorrow and everything. You should go home. Take a bath. Get some rest.

KAYLEEN: Shut up. I don't feel like walking back to my car just yet.

DOUG: Wow, you're really drunk, aren't you?

KAYLEEN: No, I'm just bleary. I feel like I just woke up.

You don't understand the week I've had.

I have to get a call at work to tell me my dad's lying dead in the driveway.

And then dealing with everyone. And this shit. And then tonight, you come riding into town. Here's Dougie, five years later all of a sudden.

I haven't slept.

I just haven't slept in like . . . I don't know. Four years or something.

Doug holds up four fingers.

DOUG: How many fingers am I holding up?

KAYLEEN: Four.

Doug holds up his middle finger.

DOUG: How about now?

KAYLEEN: Shut up.

DOUG: We can both hardly see.

Kayleen smiles at him.

KAYLEEN: Maybe that's for the best.

Long silence.

DOUG: What's gonna happen with us?

KAYLEEN: Nothing.

DOUG: Seriously.

KAYLEEN: I don't know, what?

DOUG: I don't know.

(beat) I think I'm seeing two of you.

KAYLEEN: I'm seeing two of you, too.

DOUG: Let's dance.

KAYLEEN: Shut up.

DOUG: No, we're both seeing double. We can dance, all four of us, we can play ring-around-the-rosy.

KAYLEEN: Sit down.

> *Doug pulls her up.*

KAYLEEN: I'm seriously dizzy!

DOUG: Me too!

> *They sway strangely with each other.*

DOUG: *(sings; any random melody)* Ohhh Leenie . . .
Leenie Deenie . . .
Leenie Deenie Weenie Moe.
Moe Weenie.
My Leenie Deenie Diney Doo.
Diney doo.
Diney doo.

> *They both dance and laugh.*

> *Doug takes her hand and puts it over his face.*

DOUG: Will you touch it?

KAYLEEN: What?

DOUG: My eye.

KAYLEEN: You don't have an eye.

DOUG: My eye socket.

KAYLEEN: That's disgusting.

She stops dancing with him and leans against the bed.

KAYLEEN: I probably can't smoke in here, right?

DOUG: Will you touch it?

KAYLEEN: What are you talking about. Stop being weird.

DOUG: You've always been able to mend my wounds.

KAYLEEN: Great. Glad I could've been of service.
(she takes out pack of cigarettes) I'm just going to smoke. What are they going to do?

DOUG: I know it's probably superstition, but I kind of need it. You know you always do it.

KAYLEEN: I don't always do anything.

DOUG: You've got like superpowers.
Even tonight. When we kissed, you kissed my missing tooth. The gap. And it stopped hurting.

KAYLEEN: Well I'm not touching your disgusting eye socket.

> *Doug starts to pick at the bandages around his head.*

KAYLEEN: What are you doing?

DOUG: You'll do it. You'll touch it. You'll heal me. The pills only last so long.

KAYLEEN: Stop that.

DOUG: Once the pills wear off, it's going to kill again. You've got to just touch it.

KAYLEEN: Doug, stop doing that!

> *Doug starts unpeeling the bandages around his face. He unpeels the top layer, and then starts unwrapping another layer.*

DOUG: It's okay. I know what I'm doing, okay?

KAYLEEN: I really don't want to see this!

DOUG: I just need you to help me out, Leenie. You know. You know what you do.

> *It's all off except for an extremely bloody gauze pad taped over his left eye. It looks ghoulish, disgusting, frightening.*

DOUG: Will you please touch my eye?

KAYLEEN: Get away from me! Doug, I can't look at that! Please?! Put your . . . Put that stuff back over it! This can't be healthy, come on!

DOUG: You can make it better.

KAYLEEN: No, no I can't. Leave me alone.

DOUG: Just touch it! Once!

KAYLEEN: *(with fury)* No! I will not!
   I'm not here to *take care of you*, Doug.
   I am not a *healer*.

DOUG: I'm in pain, do you understand that?!

KAYLEEN: I don't care!

DOUG: *Then leave! Get out of here, fucking go!*

> *For an instant they are both startled. Then she exits.*
>
> *Lights shift. Music fills and Kayleen and Doug prepare for scene three.*

Scene 3. Thirteen: The Limbo

> *Ten years earlier. The kids are thirteen.*
>
> *The nurse's office. Night.*
>
> *Kayleen enters. She is unwell. She wipes her mouth from having just coughed something up. She's unsteady. She is dressed for the eighth-grade dance.*
>
> *She lies on the bed, feet still on the floor.*

Doug enters, hopping on one foot. He sits quickly on the other bed.

DOUG: *(in pain)* Ah! Ah! Ah!

Kayleen looks up at him.

KAYLEEN: What happened to you?

DOUG: I was rocking out.

KAYLEEN: You were dancing?

DOUG: Yeah. I was all over the place.

KAYLEEN: Were you "break" dancing?

DOUG: No, man. It was the limbo.

KAYLEEN: Did you hurt your ankle?

DOUG: Yeah. What's wrong with you?

KAYLEEN: Nothing.

DOUG: I mean: What about the dance?

KAYLEEN: What about it.

DOUG: It's going on!

KAYLEEN: Big deal.

DOUG: You don't like it?

KAYLEEN: No.

DOUG: It's fun.

KAYLEEN: So go back to it.

DOUG: I jacked up my ankle.

KAYLEEN: Doing the limbo.

DOUG: Yeah, it's Mexican, you know? I was rocking out. How come you don't like it.

KAYLEEN: I just don't.

DOUG: So why'd you come?

KAYLEEN: Shut up.

> *Long beat.*

DOUG: Did you throw up blood?

KAYLEEN: What?!

DOUG: I heard Sister Boniface tell Mrs. Wheaton that you had thrown up blood.

KAYLEEN: I didn't throw up blood. I just threw up.

DOUG: You want me to get you some ginger ale?

KAYLEEN: No.
Thank you.

DOUG: I can throw up whenever I want.

KAYLEEN: That's reassuring.

DOUG: Really, though. I don't need to like stick my finger down my throat or anything. I can just do it, if I want.

KAYLEEN: Why would you want to.

DOUG: Sometimes, you know, just to feel better. Or, like to gross people out, or something. I was playing hockey? I play hockey. I was playing and this dude on the other team, he was a real agitator. And he kept creeping all over me, he was annoying you know? He was just annoying. And so I made myself throw up a little bit in my mouth? And I spat it on him.

KAYLEEN: That is the most disgusting thing I've ever heard in my life. You're disgusting.

DOUG: Man! He got so grossed out he started to cry. And then I was like, skating all over the place. I scored a goal. We lost, but I still scored a goal.

KAYLEEN: Hockey sounds like a wonderful activity.

DOUG: I tore my Achilles tendon last summer.

KAYLEEN: Why are you talking to me right now? Why don't you go back to your dance?

DOUG: But that's why I just hurt my ankle. It never really healed right, I think. Sometimes I hurt it just by walking.
     Do you know how I did it?

KAYLEEN: You said: dancing.

DOUG: No, I mean tore my tendon.

KAYLEEN: I don't know. Playing hockey?

DOUG: Nope. Uh-uh. I was riding on the handlebars. Todd Scott was riding and I was on the handlebars and we were speeding down the Noble Road hill and my foot got caught in the spokes and I got flipped off the bike. I also got ten stitches in my face. But also, I tore my Achilles tendon.
     I'm accident prone. That's what my mom says I am.

KAYLEEN: If you're riding on the handlebars of a bike going down a hill, you're not accident prone, you're retarded.

DOUG: You shouldn't say "retarded." That's real rude to retarded people.

KAYLEEN: Sorry I offended you.

DOUG: No, it's cool.

> *The pulse of music can be heard echoing in the distance.*

DOUG: *(nodding his head with music)* Aw yeah.
     I like this one. You wanna dance?

KAYLEEN: What are you talking about.

> *Doug gets up, gimpy, but spirited. He starts to dance awkwardly.*

DOUG: Let's dance!

KAYLEEN: Yeah right.

DOUG: I'm serious! I wanna dance with you. Get it up!

KAYLEEN: I'm not dancing!

DOUG: Come on!

> *Doug pulls her off the bed and they very awkwardly dance to the distant music. But it's too awkward and Kayleen walks away and flops on the bed.*

DOUG: What?

KAYLEEN: So! Retarded!

DOUG: How come you don't like to dance?

KAYLEEN: Would you just leave me alone?

DOUG: Go up with me.

KAYLEEN: I'm not going back to the dance, okay? Leave me alone.

DOUG: But it's fun.

KAYLEEN: It's not fun for me.

> *Doug stares at her for a moment.*
>
> *He sits, takes off his shoe, and starts scratching the bottom of his foot vigorously.*

KAYLEEN: What are you *doing*?

DOUG: Got an itchy foot.

KAYLEEN: That's disgusting.

DOUG: So? So is throwing up blood.

KAYLEEN: I didn't throw up blood.

> *Doug continues scratching his foot. Kayleen watches him, unguarded, for a moment. Then she turns away.*

DOUG: So . . . Kaitlin . . . Who do you like?

KAYLEEN: What did you just call me?

DOUG: Kaitlin.

KAYLEEN: My name is Kayleen.

DOUG: Oh, yeah, Kayleen. I meant to say Kayleen.

KAYLEEN: You're a dick.

DOUG: I am not.

KAYLEEN: Shut up.

> *Doug takes off his other shoe. He scratches that foot,*
> *but not nearly as vigorously.*

DOUG: So who do you like?

KAYLEEN: *(irritated)* I don't understand the question.

DOUG: Which guy do you like?

KAYLEEN: I hate everybody.

DOUG: Why?

KAYLEEN: I just do. Shut up.

> *Doug stops scratching his feet. He looks at them.*
> *Stretches. He takes off his socks.*

DOUG: Hey Kayleen.

KAYLEEN: What.

DOUG: Look!

> *Kayleen looks at him and he whips one of his socks*
> *at her face.*

KAYLEEN: *(totally skeeved)* Ew! Ew! That's so gross!

DOUG: It's my sock!

KAYLEEN: I know!

DOUG: It's stanky! It's smelly!

KAYLEEN: That's the grossest thing I've ever seen! You are disgusting! Get away from me!

DOUG: *Who do you like?*

KAYLEEN: Just go away!

DOUG: There's not one guy you like?

KAYLEEN: I told you, *no*. Leave me alone.

> *Doug goes and picks up his sock and takes it back to his bed.*

KAYLEEN: You're so stupid.

DOUG: I like Erin Marks.

KAYLEEN: Good for you.

DOUG: She's really pretty. I danced with her tonight. She kissed Dan Strauss.

KAYLEEN: Yeah, she also kissed Ian McGee.

DOUG: She did?

KAYLEEN: Yes.

> *Doug thinks about this.*

DOUG: She did not.

KAYLEEN: I saw them kissing backstage at the choir concert.

DOUG: Have you ever kissed anyone?

KAYLEEN: You are so stupid.

DOUG: I am not. Have you?

KAYLEEN: Shut up.

> *Doug is quiet for a moment. He goes and gets his other sock. He puts both socks back on.*

DOUG: I haven't ever kissed anyone.

KAYLEEN: I don't care.

DOUG: I'm going to kiss Erin Marks tonight.

KAYLEEN: Good for you.

Doug lies down on the bed. He stretches.

KAYLEEN: Why don't you just go back up there?

DOUG: I'm gonna go in a second.

Kayleen lies down. They both face the ceiling.

DOUG: I think kissing is going to be really nice.

KAYLEEN: You're retarded.

Doug starts kissing his forearm and the crook of his arm, as if to practice. He gets more and more passionate, trying to annoy Kayleen.

DOUG: Mmm. Kiss. Kissy kiss. Kissy kiss kiss.

Kayleen gets up to leave.

KAYLEEN: I'm leaving. You are so annoying and stupid.

DOUG: I'm not stupid. That's really mean, you know? Everyone just thinks just because I'm awesome at sports and I always get hurt that I'm stupid, but I'm not stupid, I'm just brave, that's all. I'm brave. Don't leave.

KAYLEEN: I thought you wanted to go back to the dance.

DOUG: Not yet. I want to sit here.

Kayleen goes back and sits down.

DOUG: I'm not always brave.

KAYLEEN: Yeah. I know.

Beat.

DOUG: Do you want to practice kissing?

KAYLEEN: *What?*

DOUG: I'm just saying: I never kissed anyone. And I'm assuming you haven't either. And I'm nervous about doing it, and you probably are too, so why don't we just practice so when we do have our first kiss, we'll know what we're doing.

KAYLEEN: No thank you.

DOUG: Come on.

KAYLEEN: No.

DOUG: Come on.

KAYLEEN: No, I'm not going to kiss you! That's gross!
And besides, we wouldn't have a "first kiss" after that. That would *be* our "first kiss." And I don't want my first kiss to be with you.
And I just threw up anyhow.

DOUG: It wouldn't be our first kiss, it would be a practice kiss. I don't like you, I like Erin Marks.

KAYLEEN: I just threw up.

DOUG: Didn't you wash out your mouth?

KAYLEEN: Yeah.

DOUG: So that's okay then. Come on.

He stands up.

DOUG: Kayleen, come on. Practice kiss. Then we go back up to the dance.

KAYLEEN: I can't even believe you're talking about this.

DOUG: Come on. Practice kiss.

KAYLEEN: This is just weird.
Let's just go back to the dance.

> *Kayleen gets up. Doug leans in. His face hovers just in front of hers. She looks at him, then allows Doug to kiss her. They kiss. Then they step apart.*

> *They look at each other for a moment. Kayleen puts her hand over her mouth.*

DOUG: What's wrong?

> *She's going to puke. She grabs a trash can and throws up in it. She throws up a lot.*

> *When she's done, she just stands there, holding the trash can.*

DOUG: Are you okay?

> *Kayleen won't look at him. She's clearly humiliated.*

DOUG: Kayleen, you okay?

KAYLEEN: Just please go.

> *Doug looks at her. She holds the trash can close to her body.*

> *Doug cocks his head back and makes a really strange sound, like a deep groan or gargle. He keeps doing this and then grabs the trash can from Kayleen and he throws up into it.*

> *When he's done he shakes his head, as if to clear it. And he stares into the trash can.*

DOUG: Our throw up is all mixed together.
(looks at Kayleen) You wanna see?

> *Kayleen stares at him, and then steps to him and she and Doug look in the trash can together.*

DOUG: So awesome.

KAYLEEN: Yeah. Yeah.

> *Lights shift. Music fills and Kayleen and Doug prepare for scene four.*

Scene 4. Twenty-eight: Tuesday

> *Fifteen years later. The kids are twenty-eight.*
>
> *Hospital. Doug is in a coma. He wears an eye patch over his left eye.*
>
> *Kayleen enters. She hasn't seen him like this.*

KAYLEEN: *(to herself)* Goddamnit.

> *She goes to Doug. Only beeping and other artificial sounds. She looks at him for a long time.*

KAYLEEN: Hey again.

> *Kayleen covers her face with her hands and then she exits.*
>
> *She reenters quickly.*

KAYLEEN: So I'm trying to get more healthy. Mostly. Most of the time. I thought you should know.
  So, you know, don't worry about me or anything.
  (a long moment) Come on, Doug. Wake up now. Just wake up. I'm here. I'm here to wake you up, okay? It's been a long time, I know, and I just want to . . .

> *Kayleen shakes her head, realizing she's basically talking to herself.*

KAYLEEN: Jesus. What the fuck am I doing here?

> *She goes into her bag and gets some pills. She takes*

*them. She sits down in a chair that's not close to the
bed.*

KAYLEEN: I'm so sick of your shit.

> *Kayleen rubs her temples. She gets up and walks to
> him quickly.*

KAYLEEN: *Who gets struck by fucking lightning?!*

> *She goes back to her seat and collapses in it.*

KAYLEEN: *On their fucking roof!*
I hate to tell you this, you stupid fucking genius, but getting up
on the roof in the middle of a fucking electrical storm isn't a brilliant
fucking move!

> *Kayleen calms herself. She takes out a bottle of
> lotion and pours some on her hands.*

KAYLEEN: I'm trying not to swear so much.
And I'm moisturizing.
So that's what's going on with me these days.

> *She rubs lotion into her hands.*

KAYLEEN: So congratulations on almost being married.
I mean, I heard about it.
I heard about her.
Elaine.
Elaine.
She sounds lovely. Poor girl.
You probably made the right decision, though. I don't think you're
gonna be ready to settle down till you stop climbing up on the roof,
you know? I mean, I'm no model citizen, but I do know basic fucking
things about personal safety you dumb piece of shit.

> *Kayleen puts her lotion back in her bag. She gets up
> and walks over to Doug again.*

KAYLEEN: I mean, you're not the first groom to get cold feet.

> *Kayleen shakes her head and wanders around the room.*

KAYLEEN: I feel like an idiot here.
I was pretty sure, I'd get here, say two words to you and you'd snap out of this shit. Because it's me! It's *Kayleen, Dougie!* I'm *back!*
Last time I saw you you'd just blown out your stupid eye.
It was this same hospital.

> *She goes back to her chair.*

KAYLEEN: Twice in ten years. Not stellar for a couple of kids supposed to be best friends. Twice!
Well, I guess this is three times.
Does this count? Does it count if one of us might be brain-dead?
Of course you've always been brain-dead, haven't you, Dougie? Ha, ha, ha.

> *Kayleen rubs her face.*

KAYLEEN: What else what else what else what else . . . ?

> *Kayleen gets up and looks at Doug. She slowly walks to him and touches his hand. She takes his hand in hers. This is the first time in this scene she's really let herself look at him.*
>
> *She gingerly holds out her hands over him, as if she had the power to raise the dead but knows she looks ridiculous. She touches his chest and then lifts her hands up as if she might have just woken him. Nothing.*

KAYLEEN: I am retarded.

> *She walks in a circle, and then comes back to him. She stares at him for a long moment.*

She holds his hand, rubs it. She goes to her bag, gets out the lotion, comes back to him.

KAYLEEN: Your hand is all dry.

She moisturizes his hand.

KAYLEEN: You can't marry that girl, Doug. You can't. Because what about me? What about me, huh?
    When my dad died, when you . . . when you came to the funeral home that night . . .
    That stuff you said to me . . .
    You're always doing that, you know? The top ten best things anyone's ever done for me have all been done by you.
    That's pretty good, right?
    And I know. I know I know I know . . .
    I'm so stupid. I'm always . . .
    I'm just fucked up, you know that.
    And so I need you to stick it out, Dougie.
    I'm gonna need you to come looking for me again.
    I'm sorry. But you have to wake up now. You have to wake up for me. Because I'm *not* great, you know?
    I'm not great.
    And I really need you right now. I really need you to come over and show me some stupid shit again, tell me some stupid joke like you always do.
    I'm sorry I've been gone. I'm back now. You know? I'm back now. So wake up.
    Wake up now, buddy.
    Just, you know . . . rise and shine.
    It's Tuesday.
    That was always your favorite day.

> *Lights shift. Music fills and Kayleen and Doug prepare for scene five.*

Scene 5. Eighteen: Pinkeye

Ten years earlier. The kids are eighteen.

Kayleen's bedroom. Kayleen sits on her bed, knees to her chest. Doug enters. He's beaten up pretty badly. He carries an enormous hockey duffel bag. He's in pain. He drops the bag, collapses against her bed, and yells in pain.

KAYLEEN: What are you *doing?*

DOUG: Had to stop by.

KAYLEEN: What *happened?*

DOUG: Tom Zauler happened.

KAYLEEN: What do you mean?

DOUG: I got in a fight with him.

KAYLEEN: *(very concerned)* You got in a fight with *Tom Zauler?*

DOUG: Yeah. And then that stupid Girl Scout gave me pinkeye.

He takes Girl Scout cookies out of his bag and throws them at Kayleen.

DOUG: Here. I bought her stupid cookies. Girl Scouts. What a bunch of little bitches.

KAYLEEN: These are Samoas.

DOUG: Damn right.

KAYLEEN: Where are the Thin Mints?

DOUG: Fuck that.

KAYLEEN: Fuck you.

DOUG: What's *your* problem?

KAYLEEN: Go home. I'm sick. And you're annoying. I wanted Thin Mints.

DOUG: Shut up or I'll give you pinkeye.

KAYLEEN: Go away.

> *Doug gets up, starts rubbing his eyes. And then walks to her like Frankenstein.*

DOUG: Give . . . pinkeye . . . mmmmmh . . .

KAYLEEN: Ew! Stop! Get away!

> *Doug crawls all over her on the bed. Kayleen fights him off.*

KAYLEEN: Get *off me*, you pervert!

DOUG: *Pinkeye!*

KAYLEEN: *(very serious)* Get off! God!

DOUG: What? What's wrong with you?

KAYLEEN: You're a fucking pervert! Every guy in the world! You all act like you're playing around, except you have to crawl all over me! You think I don't know you have a total hard-on right now, you perv!

DOUG: I do not!

KAYLEEN: You do too!

DOUG: I'm wearing a cup!

> *Doug knocks on his crotch. It's plastic.*

DOUG: It's a protective cup, you paranoid little horn dog.

KAYLEEN: Just leave me alone.

DOUG: Fine.

> *Doug sits down and opens cookies. He eats.*

DOUG: Ho bag.

KAYLEEN: Shut up.

DOUG: Enjoy the pinkeye. It's like the most contagious thing in the entire world.

KAYLEEN: I don't care.

DOUG: What's wrong with you anyway.

KAYLEEN: Nothing. I just am tired.
   What happened with Zauler.

DOUG: First, I punched him in the face.

KAYLEEN: Why?

Doug shrugs.

KAYLEEN: It's *Tom Zauler*, Dougie. You don't go punching Tom Zauler in the face. What do you have, a death wish?

DOUG: He threw me down and kicked me and whaled all over me. But I didn't care. I can take it. Fuckin pussy.

KAYLEEN: Why did you pick a fight with him anyhow?

DOUG: How come you weren't at school? Are you sick again?

KAYLEEN: I'm always sick.

DOUG: You don't look sick.

KAYLEEN: I'm not. Not right this minute, anyhow.

DOUG: But you sure look weird. And you're all rude and everything.

KAYLEEN: Probably cause I totally had sex today.

Doug chokes on his cookie.

DOUG: What?

KAYLEEN: With Tim.

DOUG: You had . . .
   Today!? When? How? What are you talking about?

KAYLEEN: He's my boyfriend.

DOUG: So? I know!

KAYLEEN: So we have sex!

DOUG: You mean . . . you've been *having* sex? How long?!

KAYLEEN: Like two weeks. We did it two weeks ago.

DOUG: How come you didn't tell me?

KAYLEEN: I'm telling you now!

DOUG: Well what the fuck!?

KAYLEEN: *What?*

DOUG: I don't want you having sex with *Tim!*

KAYLEEN: He's my boyfriend!

DOUG: You're too young!

KAYLEEN: Just because you've never had sex.

DOUG: I told you I did have sex.

KAYLEEN: With your cousin.

DOUG: *We're not cousins, we're family friends!*
Shut up!
I can't believe you had sex with *Tim.* That guy is nasty.

KAYLEEN: It's not like we've been doing it nonstop anyway. We only had sex twice.

DOUG: Twice?

KAYLEEN: Once two weeks ago. And then today.

DOUG: *Today?* Here?! In this bed? *Eww!* I was just in this bed that you were screwing Tim Reilly in? That guy is skeeze central.

KAYLEEN: Just forget about it then.

DOUG: I can't just forget about it!

KAYLEEN: It wasn't . . .

DOUG: . . . What?

KAYLEEN: Nothing.

DOUG: *What?*

KAYLEEN: Nothing. I just.
It's over anyway. I mean.
I did it. Twice. I got that over with.

DOUG: Sounds like it was really fun.

KAYLEEN: It wasn't, okay?
It wasn't fun.
It was . . .
It was just like, you know. Like you have to pretend you're not even doing anything, like you're just playing around, like you were with me, just now. Tim's over here, and we have to pretend like we're just being normal, you know, playing around, wrestling around and everything and then suddenly we're not, suddenly he's like . . . you know . . .

DOUG: He's like what?

KAYLEEN: Nothing.

DOUG: You didn't *want* to?

KAYLEEN: I mean . . . not at that exact moment . . .

Doug stands up, stares at her.

DOUG: Kayleen . . .

KAYLEEN: Don't get all crazy. You're always so dramatic.

DOUG: I'm going to fucking kill him.

KAYLEEN: No you're not.

DOUG: I'm gonna kick him in his ugly skull, that dirty piece of shit.

KAYLEEN: You're not going to do that.

DOUG: Why not?

KAYLEEN: Because you can't beat Tim up.
Tim will beat you up.

DOUG: *(starting to lose it)* I'm talking about you, Kayleen! I'm talking about you, and nobody can just come around and . . .
>   I'm gonna kill him. I'm gonna kill him.
>   I'm gonna fucking kill him . . . I'm gonna kill him . . .

KAYLEEN: Will you shut up *please*? Will you just sit here?

DOUG: *No I'm not going to sit down!*

KAYLEEN: He's my boyfriend!

DOUG: No he's not! Not anymore! I hate him I hate him I hate him so much . . .

>   *Doug puts his face in his hands.*

KAYLEEN: Doug . . .
>   Doug, come on.
>   Are you crying?

DOUG: *(not removing his hands; crying)* No.

>   *Kayleen grabs his shirt and pulls him to the bed*
>   *where he sits, face still in hands.*
>
>   *Kayleen hugs him.*
>
>   *Doug wipes his eyes.*

DOUG: *(quietly)* I'm gonna kill him.

KAYLEEN: No you're not.

DOUG: Why's everyone got to be so mean? Zauler . . . Tim . . . they don't . . . They're all . . .
>   Such . . .
>   Why's everyone got to be so mean?

KAYLEEN: What.

DOUG: Zauler called you a skank.
>   *(beat)* You're not a skank.
>   You're not.

They sit for a moment. He looks at her and then at
her hands. He strokes her leg in a tender way.

DOUG: You got blood on your jeans.

KAYLEEN: It's not blood.

DOUG: Yeah it is.
Yeah it is.

He looks at her.

DOUG: When you start that again?

KAYLEEN: I didn't start anything.

Doug looks at her. She looks away.

KAYLEEN: I thought having sex would, you know. A "release." Release
from what?
No release.
I thought it might make me stop.

DOUG: Does it hurt?

KAYLEEN: A little.

DOUG: What could make you stop?

KAYLEEN: I don't know. Nothing.

Doug gets up and walks away from her. Kayleen
watches him. She unbuttons her jeans and pulls
them down. Her thighs have small cuts on them.

KAYLEEN: Look.

Doug looks at her legs. He goes to her. He kneels in
front of her and lightly touches them.

DOUG: You think I could give your legs pinkeye?

KAYLEEN: Maybe.

DOUG: Yeah. Maybe.

> *Doug studies her legs.*

DOUG: What do you use?

> *Kayleen takes a box cutter from underneath her pillow.*

DOUG: If it hurts, why do you do it?

KAYLEEN: I don't know.

> *Doug touches her legs gently.*
>
> *They look at each other.*

KAYLEEN: Don't tell me to stop.

> *Doug stands up and unbuttons his pants. He pulls them down. He holds his thigh out to her.*

KAYLEEN: I'm not going to cut you.

DOUG: I won't tell you to stop if you do.

KAYLEEN: Why.

DOUG: Just do it. Just like how *you* do it.

> *Kayleen puts the box cutter to his thigh, but doesn't cut him.*

KAYLEEN: I can't.

DOUG: Do it.

KAYLEEN: Dougie, why?

DOUG: Just do it. I want to see what it's like, okay?

KAYLEEN: It's different. I can't do it to someone else.

DOUG: I'm not someone else. I'm you.

> *She looks at him. She puts the box cutter to his thigh. She cuts him. He breathes sharply, once.*

KAYLEEN: I'm sorry . . .

> *He touches his cut.*
>
> *He kneels back down in front of her. He puts his hands on her thighs. She puts her hands on top of his hands.*
>
> *They look at each other.*

DOUG: You're the prettiest girl I've ever seen.

KAYLEEN: I know.

> *Lights shift. Music fills and Kayleen and Doug prepare for scene six.*

Scene 6. Thirty-three: A Blue Raspberry Dip

> *Fifteen years later. The kids are thirty-three.*
>
> *A sterile lounge in a health facility.*
>
> *Kayleen sits in a chair, staring into space.*
>
> *Doug enters. He walks with a cane and a pronounced limp. He wears an eye patch.*
>
> *He sees her before she sees him.*

DOUG: Leenie.

> *She doesn't notice.*

DOUG: *(louder)* Kayleen.

> *She turns to see him.*

KAYLEEN: I thought you were dead.

DOUG: I wasn't.

KAYLEEN: You woke up.

DOUG: Yeah.

KAYLEEN: When?

DOUG: Five years ago.

KAYLEEN: Five years?

DOUG: Yeah.

KAYLEEN: You really woke up five years ago? Where have you been?

DOUG: I don't know.

Beat.

KAYLEEN: What's with the cane?

DOUG: Nothing.

KAYLEEN: Come on, what happened?

Doug shrugs.

KAYLEEN: Did you ever marry that girl?

DOUG: Elaine?

KAYLEEN: *Elaine.*

DOUG: You heard about that?

KAYLEEN: Yeah.

DOUG: No.

KAYLEEN: I thought you were dead.

DOUG: Did you visit me?

KAYLEEN: They've got me on about twenty-five medications or something. Like a swirl of ice cream in me. You know how they dip the ice cream and it gets a hardened shell?

DOUG: Like at the Frostee Freeze.

KAYLEEN: I'm a blue raspberry dip.

DOUG: Delicious.

KAYLEEN: Yeah.
(beat) This place isn't too bad. Except for the food and you can't smoke.
(beat) I had a bad patch, Dougie.

DOUG: What did you do?

KAYLEEN: I hurt myself.

DOUG: How.

KAYLEEN: I don't remember doing it.

DOUG: Doing what?

KAYLEEN: My stomach. You know, it always hurt. And my mom, and all that.
And it got worse, and I just tried to take it out.

DOUG: What do you mean.

KAYLEEN: I was out of my head. I tried to cut my stomach out.

Beat. Doug flinches.

DOUG: That sort of thing. It's not healthy.

KAYLEEN: It was okay. I'm not very good with a knife.

DOUG: Kayleen . . .
You visited me didn't you? In the hospital?
Because I swear to God I heard your voice out there.
Or your presence or, what, your echo . . . I don't know how, but I remember you, something about you . . . coming to me, and sinking into me, and giving me breath again.
You came and healed me.

KAYLEEN: What does it matter?

DOUG: What do you mean what does it matter? You raised me from the dead!

KAYLEEN: No, I *did not!*

I'm not your guardian fucking angel, Doug, for God's sake look at me, okay? I didn't come and see you.

DOUG: No. No no no, you can't lie to me. I can see it all over your face, you were there. You were *there.*

KAYLEEN: *(with rage) I wasn't fucking there!*

DOUG: *(angry; slams cane)* Well why *not?*

KAYLEEN: Because why would I, Doug? What about when *I* needed somebody?! Where were *you* the last five years?

DOUG: My life got away from me.

KAYLEEN: Poor you.

DOUG: Every angle of it.
I probably have ten thousand excuses, but I . . .
Kayleen, I'm sorry.
Something happened to me and I had to find you.
Look . . .

> *Doug goes into his bag and takes out a small stone statue of an owl.*

DOUG: I brought you this.

KAYLEEN: What is it?

DOUG: You don't remember?

KAYLEEN: No.

DOUG: You don't remember this owl.

KAYLEEN: *No.*

DOUG: Yes you do.

KAYLEEN: Am I supposed to?

DOUG: Stop *lying!*

KAYLEEN: I'm *not!*

DOUG: You know this owl! We used to think it was an angel, back at school! It was a small statue on the roof of St. Margaret Mary's.

KAYLEEN: I don't remember.

DOUG: You're full of *shit!*

KAYLEEN: I don't remember anything okay? I'm sorry! How'd you get it?

DOUG: St. Margaret Mary's blew up.

KAYLEEN: *What?*

DOUG: It exploded.

KAYLEEN: Were there kids in it?

DOUG: No, you idiot. It closed down like ten years ago.
It was used by the diocese for storage. There was a leaking gas main. *Ka-Boom.*

KAYLEEN: So what, you went to pick through the rubble?

DOUG: No, I work in insurance now.

KAYLEEN: *What.*

DOUG: I'm a claims adjuster.

KAYLEEN: You're such a loser.

DOUG: I know.
But I got to go and investigate the wreckage.
I go over and the place is collapsed. So I hoist myself up there and I'm walking on the roof and then I stepped through a weak board or something and this upright nail went clear through my foot. It was about eight inches long.
Then the board with the nail in it, *that* board snapped through another board and I broke my leg in three places.
It took them five hours to get me out.
And then I got an infection.
And that's why I have this cane now.
But listen: I'm up there, you know? Stuck up there, waiting for them to come and get me.

And there were these severed heads of a bunch of saints that had ended up all over the place, and they were just staring at me.

And this owl was there too.

And so I lean over and grab the little guy.

I was in some serious pain, you know? And I just gripped him close to me, because . . .

Because all of a sudden, I was like, *Where the fuck is Kayleen?*

You know? All of a sudden, everything was clear . . . trapped up on that roof, impaled, surrounded by all the angels and saints . . .

That's my life, up there, Leenie. That's my life without you.

> *Beat.*

KAYLEEN: Does it hurt?

DOUG: It's stigmata!

KAYLEEN: It's not stigmata, it's one foot. Stigmata is both feet and both hands. Let's keep perspective.

DOUG: It hurts a little.

> *Long beat. Kayleen holds the owl and looks at him.*

KAYLEEN: Look at this poor guy. He's all beat-up.

DOUG: Spent his whole life up there on that roof. Looking down.

> *Beat.*

KAYLEEN: Do you want to touch my scar?

> *Doug doesn't answer. They stare at each other for a moment. She gets up and goes to him.*
>
> *She pulls her shirt out so Doug can put his hand up her shirt. He does, and touches her stomach.*

DOUG: God, Leenie.

KAYLEEN: That's my scar, Dougie. It's like a roller coaster across my stomach. You're not the only retardo on the planet.

She tenderly touches his head. He takes her face in his hands. His hand remains up her shirt.

KAYLEEN: You didn't even like him. You said he was a stupid-looking angel.

DOUG: You do remember.

KAYLEEN: Yes, goddamnit, I remember my goddamn angel.

They sway together for a moment.

DOUG: I wish I could do to you what you do to me.
(*beat*) I wish you'd let me.
(*beat*) Hey. Look at me.
I'd been up on that roof before.

KAYLEEN: I know.

DOUG: The day we met.
You cleaned the grit out of my hands.

KAYLEEN: I know.

DOUG: You think we could get out of here?
You think we could just pry ourselves out of everything?
Go somewhere else?

KAYLEEN: Somewhere else.

DOUG: Yeah. Anywhere.

KAYLEEN: I can't.

DOUG: Not even right this minute. Sometime soon, I could come and get you and . . .

KAYLEEN: I can't.
I can't.

Kayleen steps away from him. She stops looking at him. She sits back down, holding the owl.

DOUG: Will you look me?
Kayleen, look at me for one second.

She doesn't. He stares at her. She holds the owl,
staring at it. A long beat. He realizes she won't look
at him.

DOUG: Are you going to let me drift away here? Because I don't want to, Leens. I'm worn out. I don't have so much left in me anymore you know?
I'm saying, don't let me. Don't let me drift away again.
I might not make it back.

> *Lights shift. Music fills and Kayleen and Doug*
> *prepare for scene seven.*

Scene 7. Twenty-three: Tooth and Nail

> *Ten years earlier. The kids are twenty-three.*

> *Night, outside of a funeral home. Kayleen sits on*
> *the steps of the funeral home, smoking. She wears*
> *the same black dress from scene two, but she looks*
> *clean and sober.*

> *Doug enters. He's wearing the black suit from scene*
> *two, but no blood, and he still has his left eye. He's*
> *missing one of his front teeth.*

> *They look at each other.*

DOUG: *(smiles)* Hey again.

KAYLEEN: What happened to your tooth?

DOUG: Knocked it out. This morning. I was hammering in the shed.
Hi Kayleen.

KAYLEEN: Hey again.

DOUG: I'm sorry.

KAYLEEN: For what.

DOUG: For your dad.

KAYLEEN: You're sorry for him.

DOUG: *About* him.

KAYLEEN: You missed the wake. Everyone went home. No one in there but a dead guy in a box.

DOUG: I thought it went till nine.

KAYLEEN: Eight-thirty.

DOUG: It's good to see you.

KAYLEEN: Fuck off. Toothless piece of shit.

> *They smile at each other. Doug goes to her for a hug.*

DOUG: It's so good to see you.

KAYLEEN: No, don't hug me. I'm all hugged out. I've been hugging people all day. Everyone in here: *I'm sorry for your loss. I'm so sorry for your loss.*
What loss?
If I hug one more person I'm going to choke on my own spit.

DOUG: It's been forever, Leenie.

KAYLEEN: I've been here. Where the fuck have you been?

DOUG: College.

KAYLEEN: College.

DOUG: I came back in the summers and Christmas. I tried to find you. I tried to look you up, but I couldn't find you.

KAYLEEN: I was here.

DOUG: Where? Not listed. Not at home.

KAYLEEN: I work. I work and I sleep. What do you do?

DOUG: Nothing. Not right now. Looking. I don't know. Seems whenever I'm home I'm looking for you.

KAYLEEN: You didn't look hard enough.

> *Doug shakes himself out, as if waking from a dream or a trance.*

DOUG: Jeez, Leenie, you're here now! I found you!

> *He sits next to her and hugs her. She's annoyed.*

KAYLEEN: Would you stop? You're a freak.

DOUG: I missed you. I missed you, Leenie.

KAYLEEN: Don't call me that. Nobody calls me that.

DOUG: I call you that.
What are you smoking?

KAYLEEN: Cigarettes.

DOUG: Give me one.

KAYLEEN: Since when do you smoke.

DOUG: I don't.

> *She gives him one and they both light a cigarette and smoke.*

DOUG: So what's been going on with you for the last four years?

> *She moves away from him.*

KAYLEEN: No, let's not do that. I don't feel like recapping the last four years of my life.

DOUG: Fine.

> *Beat.*

KAYLEEN: I'm waiting tables.

DOUG: Your dad told me you were waitressing.

> *She looks at him, not expecting this.*

DOUG: I told you, I came looking for you.

KAYLEEN: You talked to my dad?

DOUG: I came by your place.

KAYLEEN: When?

DOUG: This was like a year ago. I stopped to see if you were there. I talked to your dad. He told me you were waitressing but he didn't know where.

KAYLEEN: You *talked* to my dad?

DOUG: You think I enjoyed that? I hated being in the same room with that guy.
     May he rest in peace.

> *Beat.*

KAYLEEN: He never told me you stopped by.

DOUG: Big surprise there.

KAYLEEN: He's such an asshole.
     (beat) I'm alone now, Dougie.

DOUG: You're not alone.

KAYLEEN: Yeah, I am. My mom died last year.

DOUG: What? She died? When? How?

KAYLEEN: I don't know. Her stomach.

DOUG: Jesus, Leenie, I'm sorry.

KAYLEEN: Yeah, I know, you're *sorry for my loss* . . . I hadn't seen her in eleven years. Her ex-boyfriend called me to give me the news. You know what my dad said when I told him?

DOUG: What?

KAYLEEN: He started crying and told me she was a better woman than I'd ever be.
     This bitch who walked out on us.

> *Beat.*

DOUG: You're not alone, Leenie.

KAYLEEN: Don't call me that.

DOUG: *Leenie.*

KAYLEEN: Shut up.

DOUG: *Leenie Deenie.*

KAYLEEN: I'm going to burn you with my cigarette.

He grins at her.

KAYLEEN: You need to get a fake tooth, like, *stat.* You look inbred. *(beat)* Did it hurt?

DOUG: It hurt like crazy.

Beat.

KAYLEEN: It's good to see you, too.

DOUG: I think I'm home now.

KAYLEEN: What's that mean?

DOUG: It means I'm home. I'm back.

KAYLEEN: Well, that's good, I guess.

DOUG: You know, whenever anything crazy happened in college, or I saw something amazing or beautiful or fucked up, I'd think, man, Leenie'd love this shit.
Sometimes I'd just imagine you were there, you know, I'd imagine you were there and I'd start having a conversation with you. Just start talking to you.

KAYLEEN: Yeah, there's a word for that and it's *schizophrenia.*

DOUG: I just want to be friends again.

KAYLEEN: You're the one who left.

DOUG: Are you okay?

KAYLEEN: I'm fine.

DOUG: Are you okay?

KAYLEEN: I told you, I'm fine.

DOUG: Come here.

KAYLEEN: No.

DOUG: Kayleen, come here.

KAYLEEN: Fuck off.

> *Doug walks to her. He takes her face in his hands.*
> *She tries to resist, but relents.*

DOUG: Look at me.

KAYLEEN: *What*, Doug.

> *They stare at each other. He kisses her. She lets him,*
> *but doesn't kiss him back.*

DOUG: I love you.

> *She pulls away from him.*

KAYLEEN: Your parents were here tonight.

DOUG: I know.

KAYLEEN: They sent flowers.
Your mother said she was going to bring by a casserole.
That's what your mom is like.
She's the kind of woman who brings over a casserole.

DOUG: They love you, too.

KAYLEEN: This is so fucked up what you're doing right now.

DOUG: What are you talking about . . . ?

KAYLEEN: Kissing me. Coming back like this. Telling me you love me,
your parents love me.
Just leave me alone.

DOUG: Leenie . . .

KAYLEEN: You're so stupid. You always think everything is one way, but you don't know anything.

DOUG: What!? What don't I know?

KAYLEEN: You don't know *me*, okay? You think I'm someone, some girl you dreamt up a million years ago.

DOUG: Well, then, who are you?

KAYLEEN: Nothing. Just shut up.

DOUG: No, who are you? Since I don't know anything, who are you?

KAYLEEN: Shut up.

> *Doug goes to her and tries to kiss her, but she steps away and doesn't let him.*

KAYLEEN: Don't.

DOUG: Why not.

> *She doesn't answer. She lights a cigarette.*

DOUG: I've got some fireworks in my car.

KAYLEEN: You're retarded.

DOUG: I do. I've got a mess of them in my trunk.
Killer, too.
The Japanese shit.

KAYLEEN: We're not going to light off fireworks.

DOUG: Why not?

KAYLEEN: I don't know, Dougie. Maybe because we're not fifteen anymore? Or because you're retarded? Or because I have to wake up tomorrow for my father's funeral?

DOUG: We'll go to the bridge down on Roanoke. Just like old times.

KAYLEEN: I'm living with someone.

DOUG: You're living with someone . . . what, like you have a roommate?

KAYLEEN: I'm living with a guy. We've been together for a year.

DOUG: Where is he? He's not with you?

KAYLEEN: He doesn't like funerals.

DOUG: He doesn't like funerals? This isn't a funeral. This is a wake.

KAYLEEN: He said seeing a dead body would wig him out.
(beat) Just shut up.

DOUG: And you're *with* this guy.

KAYLEEN: Don't judge him.
He's sensitive.

DOUG: Fuck him.
Fuck him fuck him fuck him.

KAYLEEN: That's nice.

> *Doug paces. He starts to leave. He comes back.*

DOUG: You know what, Kayleen? Jesus Christ, you know, I came to your house last year and your dad was there, and I know he hates my guts, he always has, and he's like *She is where she is. I don't know where the girl is.*
He said he didn't care and didn't care to know.
And I was about to just leave, but I didn't. I didn't and I said to that son of a bitch . . .
(he turns to the funeral home and shouts at it)
You remember, asshole? You dead piece of shit!? You remember what I said to you!?
I said to him, you are fucking *worthless.*
You have a daughter and she is a gift from God. She is the most perfect being to ever walk this earth and you don't even know it. And she loves you because you're her stupid father. But you've never loved her back, you've just damaged her and fucked her up, and never even bothered to notice she's this *angel.*
So *fuck you, cocksucker.*

(beat) And then I told him I hoped he'd die alone.
Which he did.
So I feel a little guilty about that now.
(beat) I can take care of you, Leenie.

> *Beat. He approaches her. She hasn't been looking at him, but she has been moved by his words. He reaches out and touches her face. She flinches, recoils from his touch, and steps away from him.*

KAYLEEN: I don't need anyone to take care of me.

> *Doug turns to leave.*

KAYLEEN: Where are you going.

DOUG: I'm going to go light up my fireworks.

> *He exits.*

KAYLEEN: Bye.

> *She takes out a cigarette. Lights it. Looks out after him. Sits down.*

KAYLEEN: *(more to herself)* Don't blow your face off.

> *Lights shift. Music fills and Kayleen and Doug prepare for scene eight.*

Scene 8. Thirty-eight: Zamboni

> *Fifteen years later.*
>
> *The kids are thirty-eight.*
>
> *An empty indoor ice rink. Kayleen is sitting on a bench looking out at the ice. She looks much different. She's totally cleaned up. She's dressed*

conservatively. She wears a long skirt, a sweater, a
shawl around her. She's cold.

After a moment, Doug enters. He is in a wheelchair.
He wears a coat and a knit cap, and, of course, an
eye patch.

They haven't seen each other since he visited her in
the hospital five years ago.

They look at each other but don't say anything. They
both look out at the rink.

DOUG: I did a good job with that ice.

KAYLEEN: It looks like glass.

DOUG: They rebuilt the Zam for me. I can drive it with my hands.
(beat) Last cut of the day.
It's late.

KAYLEEN: I didn't know. About you. About the accident.

Doug doesn't answer.

KAYLEEN: After I got out . . .
I was too . . .

DOUG: I don't remember anything.
I remember things.
But I don't remember things.

KAYLEEN: It's cold.

DOUG: Ice rink.
(beat) I watch the kids play hockey.
Oh, they fly around.
They fly around the rink.
(beat) I like it at night after the last cut.
Look at the ice, Kayleen.

KAYLEEN: Your mom told me I could find you here.
She's so nice to me.

As if she doesn't know anything.
Or maybe as if she knows everything.
You and your family, Dougie. Nicest people in the world.
And you have to get tangled up in the spokes of my train wreck.

DOUG: Trains don't have spokes.

> *Beat.*

KAYLEEN: Dougie . . .
Why do you do this?

> *He doesn't answer.*

KAYLEEN: Where'd you learn how to climb a telephone pole?

DOUG: Easy to climb up. Not so easy to climb down. Especially in the pouring rain.

KAYLEEN: Why did you climb it?

DOUG: You were unlisted.

KAYLEEN: You're stupid.

DOUG: Maybe.

KAYLEEN: Not maybe.

DOUG: Maybe if I could climb to the top of this telephone pole in the rain at night, like the mast of a ship lost at sea, maybe I'll see the shine of you, bringing me home again.
   (beat) That's the maybe.

KAYLEEN: *(quiet)*
That's stupid.

DOUG: But here you are.

KAYLEEN: Yeah. Here I am.

> *She looks at him; he looks at the ice. A long moment.*

KAYLEEN: I came here to lay my hands on you, Dougie. I've never believed it, but I have to do it . . . because if you believe it, that must be enough.

Doug doesn't answer, doesn't look at her.

KAYLEEN: I came and saw you when you were in the coma.

DOUG: You said you didn't.

KAYLEEN: I did. I came and saw you. I touched you. I felt like an idiot, but I did. And nothing happened, so I just felt it was stupid.
But you woke up.
You woke up, you freak.
I don't believe in any of this stuff, you know, Dougie? Energy. Healing powers. But I don't care right now. You're in a stupid wheelchair.

DOUG: How come you said you didn't come see me.

KAYLEEN: I don't know, Doug, there you were asking me if I was the reason you miraculously sprang back to life. I can't be the reason you're alive. Why would I be able to do something like that?

Doug doesn't answer, doesn't look at her.

KAYLEEN: Dougie . . .

DOUG: I did a good job with that ice.

KAYLEEN: *(getting up)* Dougie, I'm going to touch you now. Tell me where.
Tell me where.

DOUG: Don't touch me.

She stops and looks at him.

KAYLEEN: I know. But . . . I just think . . .

DOUG: Do not touch me.

KAYLEEN: I want to, Dougie. I'm sorry for . . .

I'm sorry for our whole life right now.

DOUG: Don't touch me, Kayleen.

> *Kayleen doesn't. She watches him. He won't look at her. She goes to him and crouches, puts her hands on his wheel.*

KAYLEEN: Not even for that, Dougie. For me. Just for me. Can I just . . .

> *She puts her hand up to touch his face, but can't do it.*

DOUG: *(almost desperate)* Please.

> *Kayleen stands and goes back to the bench and sits.*
>
> *She covers her face with her hands for a moment.*

DOUG: I'm good like this. I'm good. Don't need anything else. Except maybe when I see those kids flying around on the ice. But I'm done flying around.

> *Beat.*

KAYLEEN: God, I feel sick.

DOUG: Throw up.

KAYLEEN: I want to.

> *Beat.*

DOUG: Remember . . . ?

KAYLEEN: Yeah.

DOUG: What happened after.

KAYLEEN: I don't know. We stood there staring at it.

DOUG: Disgusting.

KAYLEEN: You cleaned it out.

DOUG: I did?

KAYLEEN: Yeah, you washed it out.
We left. We went out to the playground.

DOUG: We sat on the swings.

KAYLEEN: We sat on the swings.
You kept climbing up the swing chains and swinging from the top bar, like ten feet off the ground.
And I told you you were stupid and going to crack open your head.
So you came back down.
And we sat on the swings.

DOUG: What did we talk about.

KAYLEEN: God, I don't know . . .
We talked about everything. We talked so long, it was the latest I'd ever stayed up in my life.
It was almost morning when we left the swings.
It was cold, and you gave me your jacket to wear.
The playground was so pretty just then.
The sky was starting to be blue.

They look at the ice.

ANIMALS
OUT OF
PAPER

PRODUCTION HISTORY

Animals Out of Paper had its world premiere on August 4, 2008, at Second Stage Theatre in New York City. Carole Rothman, Artistic Director; Ellen Richard, Executive Director; Giovanna Sardelli, Director; Beowulf Boritt, Set Designer; Amy Clark, Costume Designer; Josh Bradford, Lighting Designer; Bart Fasbender, Sound Designer; Don-Scott Cooper, General Manager; Barlow/Hartman Public Relations, Press Representative; Lori Ann Zepp, Production Stage Manager; Stephanie Gatton, Stage Manager; Robert G. Mahon III, Production Manager; Jeremy Palmer, Technical Director; Laura Schutzel, Casting; Tara Rubin Casting, Casting.

ILANA: Kellie Overbey
ANDY: Jeremy Shamos
SURESH: Utkarsh Ambudkar

CHARACTERS

ILANA: female, forty to forty-five
ANDY: male, thirty-five to forty-five
SURESH: an eighteen-year-old Indian boy, raised in the U.S.

TIME

The present

ACT 1
Scene 1.

Dim lights illuminate the extremely messy studio apartment of Ilana Andrews, who sleeps on her couch in a bathrobe. Origami models of animals and abstract shapes fill the apartment. Also, empty bottles, large stacks of folding paper, newspapers, books, clothes strewn everywhere. There is a fire extinguisher on the kitchen counter.

Also, an enormous number of empty and used Chinese food take-out boxes.

Also, several diagrams of a human heart. Some are in color, some drawn in pencil. One is very large, with measurements drawn over the heart.

Hanging from the ceiling directly above Ilana is an enormous origami hawk, three or four times its natural size, folded in such a way that it looks like it's about to pounce on its prey. Its huge talons are wide open, hovering several feet over Ilana.

The apartment buzzer buzzes. Ilana is startled. No one ever buzzes this door. She just stares at the intercom from the couch. The door buzzes a few more times. She slowly walks to the intercom. She presses it and speaks.

ILANA: Hello?

ANDY: *(intercom)* Hello?

ILANA: Yes?

ANDY: Hi.

ILANA: Yes?

ANDY: Ilana Andrews?

ILANA: That's me . . .

ANDY: Hi.

ILANA: Can I help you?

ANDY: Andy Froling.

ILANA: Who?

ANDY: Andy Froling. American Origami.

ILANA: Is there something you need?

ANDY: Could you buzz me in?

ILANA: Who *are* you?

ANDY: Andy Froling. American Origami.

ILANA: Yeah, *I don't know you.*

ANDY: American Origami.

ILANA: What about it?

ANDY: I'm the treasurer.
   (beat) Can you buzz me in?

ILANA: Look: I don't know you.

ANDY: It's just that it's raining.

ILANA: It is?

ANDY: It's pouring. Look out the window. It's a monsoon.

ILANA: I don't have a window.

ANDY: Could you buzz me in?

ILANA: What do you want?

ANDY: I have some stuff for you. We tried mailing it to you, but it comes back. Could you buzz me in please? I'm getting soaked out here. I just need to drop this thing off.

> *Ilana paces around, nervous, not wanting to let this person in. She lets her finger off the button and*

stares at the intercom as if it was a dangerous thing.
She presses it again and Andy's been talking.

ANDY: . . . who told me he thought it looked like a lozenge or maybe a dorsal fin. But I don't know . . . it was so beautiful. Like the most beautiful thing I ever saw. I'm sorry, but I guess I just wanted to say that.

ILANA: What?

ANDY: Could you just please buzz me in?

> *Ilana goes to the couch. Leans against it for a*
> *moment. Returns.*
>
> *She presses the button again.*

ILANA: Hello?

ANDY: Hi.

ILANA: Okay.

> *Ilana takes her finger off the intercom button and*
> *just stares at the box for a long moment. And then*
> *she buzzes him in. She just stands there waiting.*
>
> *A knock on the door. Ilana opens it. Andy enters,*
> *totally drenched.*

ANDY: Hi.

ILANA: Yeah. Hi.

ANDY: Andy Froling. American Origami.

ILANA: Yeah. Hi.

ANDY: I'm the treasurer.
(*seeing the hawk, starts to enter*) Wow, that is a big bird.

ILANA: Yeah.
(*alarmed as he starts to enter*) Hey!

ANDY: What?

ILANA: I've got a lot of paper . . . There's paper . . . Like everywhere. Don't get my paper wet. Just . . . just stay right there. Don't move.

ANDY: I'm here. Not gonna move.

ILANA: Thanks.

ANDY: *(looking at the hawk)* Wow.

ILANA: Yeah.

ANDY: *Wow.*

ILANA: Yeah.

ANDY: It's so nice to see you again.

ILANA: Yeah.
When did we meet?

ANDY: The convention?

ILANA: Right.

ANDY: I'm the treasurer.

ILANA: This past June.

ANDY: Yeah . . . And the four previous Junes. I've been.

ILANA: Oh. Right . . .

ANDY: Yeah.

ILANA: Yeah.

Awkward pause.

ANDY: *(holds out a folder)* So, this is . . .

ILANA: Right!

ANDY: Yeah, just some . . .

ILANA: And this is . . . ?

ANDY: Yeah, just some . . .

ILANA: I should sign them?

ANDY: Sure. I mean, no, it's just informational. We wanted to make sure you got it. I mean, if you don't get the stuff . . . I mean, we want to make sure that you're gonna be with us again in June . . . Will you?

ILANA: Sure.

ANDY: It's just that your mail was sent back.

ILANA: I moved.

ANDY: And so . . . you live . . . *here* now . . . In your studio?

ILANA: It's temporary.

ANDY: I'm sorry for intruding.

ILANA: Sorry you got wet.

ANDY: Water's water. It doesn't hurt any. Rain is sacred, that's what I say. All water is holy water.

ILANA: Yeah?

ANDY: Why not? *Wow,* that is just a huge bird. What is that? Is that a composite?

ILANA: Yeah. There's five pieces in there.

ANDY: It looks so alive! So eaglelike!

ILANA: It's a hawk.

ANDY: A hawk! Pouncing! *Pouncing on its prey!*

ILANA: Well, it's been *great* talking to you, but . . .

ANDY: It's just so well crafted. Really phenomenal. And I love what it does to the room!

> *Ilana looks around the room and then at the bird.*

ILANA: You like it?

ANDY: I love it.

ILANA: Well, if you can get it down, you can have it.

ANDY: The hawk? Are you serious?

ILANA: I can't get it down. And I'm sick of it.

ANDY: How'd you get it up?

ILANA: My ex-husband put it up there.

ANDY: Oh.

ILANA: Yeah.

ANDY: I'm sorry.

ILANA: Don't be. Do you want the bird?

ANDY: I'd love it! *Wow!* An Ilana Andrews original! Where's your ladder?

ILANA: I don't have a ladder. If I had a ladder, I could get it down myself.

Andy looks around the room.

ANDY: Okay. If I put that ottoman on top of the couch, I think I could reach it and snip off the line. You think?

ILANA: You'll have to take off your shoes. You're going to have to dry off.

ANDY: Shoes off!

Andy pulls his shoes off.

Ilana takes a roll of paper towels and hands it to him.

ILANA: Here. Take as much as you need.

ANDY: Oh, wow. Thanks . . .

Andy takes a lot of paper towel and mops himself off, head to toe.

ANDY: This place is great. Just great.

He points to a Chinese take-out box.

ANDY: Hey did you do that? That's great.

ILANA: Those are take-out boxes.

ANDY: Oh.

ILANA: Yeah, that's Szechuan beef.

ANDY: It's just that there's so many. I thought it was conceptual.

ILANA: I haven't been out in a while.

ANDY: So you've been ordering in.
Chinese food. That's great.
I don't like it. Allergic. MSG.

ILANA: I'm getting tired of it myself.

ANDY: Yeah, you look tired.

ILANA: Thanks. Well, I am.

ANDY: It happens, you know. People get tired. I drink tea.

ILANA: You drink tea.

ANDY: When I get tired. It relaxes and energizes me *at the same time.*
Great stuff, tea. Do you have any?

ILANA: Tea? Yeah, I have tea.

ANDY: Oh, then you should drink some.

ILANA: Um. Okay. Yeah.

ANDY: Are you going to make some?

ILANA: I guess. Do you . . . uh . . . do you want some?

ANDY: I'd love some tea. Thank you.

> *He hands the large wad of soaked paper towels to
> Ilana. She takes it awkwardly and goes to a little
> kitchenette, fills two mugs with water, and then puts
> them in the microwave.*
>
> *Andy looks up at the bird.*

ANDY: Oh, she's a beauty.
And you're a genius.

ILANA: I'm not and you don't know me.

ANDY: I know your work. I took your class on the scaled koi.

ILANA: It's a fish. Anyone can fold that.

ANDY: I can't. Still can't.

ILANA: I must not have been a very good teacher.

ANDY: You were. You were a great teacher. I know, because I'm a teacher. calculus. High school. Heights High.
(fist in the air; like a school cheer) Heights Hiiigh!

ILANA: I have lemon zinger.

ANDY: Oh, that's fine. I'm a big fan of the zingers.
And by the way . . . regardless. I'm sorry about your, um, the divorce. It's just difficult to be with someone and then to not be with them.

ILANA: Have you been married?

ANDY: No, never.

ILANA: Then you don't really know, do you?

ANDY: I guess not.

ILANA: No. You don't.

ANDY: It's just that . . . we heard about it at A.O. A.O.—that's "American Origami."

ILANA: I got it.

ANDY: And then your mail got returned to us. And you never answered e-mail and your cell phone got disconnected . . . and we got sort of worried for a second there.

ILANA: Who was worried?

ANDY: Well, I was. I mean . . . I pretty much do everything anyhow.

ILANA: You don't even know me.

ANDY: I'm just saying I was worried.

ILANA: Don't worry about me.

ANDY: Okay, I won't.

ILANA: *Don't worry about me!*

ANDY: *Okay I won't.*

ILANA: I am *fine.* I'm fine, okay? *Fine. I am fine.*

ANDY: Okay.

ILANA: Don't worry about me.

ANDY: I won't.

ILANA: I'm fine.

ANDY: Yep.

ILANA: You want sugar or honey?

ANDY: Honey.

ILANA: I don't have honey.

ANDY: Sugar.

ILANA: I have enough problems, I don't need the treasurer for American Origami hunting me down to give me a *brochure.*

ANDY: It wasn't just the brochure, why I came over.

ILANA: What else?

ANDY: Your, um . . . A.O. dues? Yearly dues? They were due December first.

ILANA: Are you kidding me?

ANDY: It's no big deal! It's only twenty-five dollars!

ILANA: You came over here because I'm late on my membership dues?

ANDY: I already paid it.

ILANA: *You* paid my dues?

ANDY: It wasn't a big deal! I didn't want to bother you, but, like I said, I was worried . . .

ILANA: *Don't pay my fucking dues!*

ANDY: *Okay!*

> *Ilana storms to her purse and takes out her wallet.*

ILANA: Twenty-five bucks? Fine. Here. Here's twenty-five bucks for *American Origami.* You guys must be doing *great* if you're shaking people down for twenty-five bucks . . .

(no cash in her wallet) I don't have any cash.

Can I write you a check?

ANDY: Ilana, please, don't worry about it! I shouldn't even have brought it up!

ILANA: But you did.

ANDY: Please, just forget I said anything.

Ilana goes to get the tea.

ILANA: Unbelievable.

I crawl into a hole for two months, and the only person who notices is the treasurer from American Origami.

If I dropped dead tomorrow, my gravestone would read "She owed twenty-five dollars in dues."

She goes to him and hands him the cup.

ILANA: Here's your lemon zinger.

ANDY: Thank you. This is very nice.

Ilana goes back to her cup. She's pent up.

ILANA: My dog ran off.

ANDY: Oh . . . I'm sorry.

ILANA: I lost my dog.

ANDY: That's tough.

ILANA: Yeah, it's tough.

ANDY: Have you checked the pound?

ILANA: Shut up.

ANDY: Okay.

They drink their tea.

ILANA: He had three legs.

ANDY: Really?

ILANA: Yeah.

ANDY: It's sad when dogs only have three legs.

ILANA: He could barely walk across the kitchen floor for the past two years and then one morning he's gone. Poof. Disappeared.

ANDY: Ah.

> *They drink.*

ANDY: Lemony.

> *They drink.*

ANDY: I count my blessings.

ILANA: That's great. Good for you.

ANDY: No, I literally count my blessings. I keep them in here.

> *Andy goes into his jacket pocket and pulls out a small book with a rubber band around it.*

ANDY: When I think of one, I number it and add it to the list.

ILANA: You're kidding me.

ANDY: It's just something I do.
   (he opens it, reads) Number 1: My health.
   (looks up) That's pretty basic.
   (reads) Number 2: I can still go bowling, even with my elbow.
   Number 1,943: I like teaching and am good at teaching.
   Number 2,845: It is quiet and warm in my apartment in the morning and I can always have a cup of tea and look out my window.
   (looks up) I mean, that's a blessing! That's an honest-to-goodness blessing!

ILANA: Right.

ANDY: *(reads)* Number 3,971: Turkey jerky.
(looks up) Turkey jerky!
(he flips through) I'm at 7,904 right now. 7,904 blessings counted.

ILANA: You've counted seven thousand blessings. How long did that take?

ANDY: I started when I was twelve. I had a fortune cookie. It said, "Count your blessings."

ILANA: You're very literal, aren't you?

ANDY: Sometimes they get repeated, but that's okay, I say.
(he looks back in the book) Oh, listen to this one.
Number 5,848: *Folding What I Lost* by Ilana Andrews.

ILANA: My book?

ANDY: Yep!

ILANA: My book is one of your blessings?

ANDY: It's my favorite book. One of them, anyway. My favorite origami book.
I love that book, oh mister, yes I do. I've only read it about two hundred times! I keep extra copies around just to give to people who I like. I say: Just read this. You don't even have to fold to like this book.

ILANA: Come on . . . it's an origami book.

ANDY: *(reads)* Number 126: Origami.

ILANA: Origami.

ANDY: Number 127: The way I feel when I am folding.

> *Ilana knows what he's talking about for the first time. They look at each other. Then Andy goes back to the book.*

ANDY: Here's another one about your book.
Number 5,962: Folding Ilana's models which are the things she's lost in her life and reading her little essays about them. They are like little poems. Folding things I never lost and it makes me think about

losing things I never even had. And it is sad, but a good sad, like melancholy.

And then I have the next one.

Number 5,963: Melancholy.

(looks up) I think I was thinking that melancholy is kind of a blessing, because it's not a serious sadness, it's more like a sweet sadness and it's nice to have some melancholy and read something nice or listen to music or fold. If I wrote a book, maybe I'd call it "Melancholy Folding" or something. Not that I'd ever write a book, being that I don't write and I don't fold well enough to write a book on it, but I guess I sometimes think about it anyhow, sort of like a harmless fantasy. Boy, I'm talking a lot. I'm sorry. Sometimes I talk and I forget to stop. Sorry. I'll shut up.

> *Awkward silence. Andy looks up at the bird.*

ANDY: I can really have that?

ILANA: If you can get it down.

> *Andy looks around the room.*
>
> *Andy puts his little book on a table.*
>
> *He picks up the ottoman and puts it on the couch.*

ANDY: It's like making a fort!

ILANA: Yeah. A fort.

ANDY: *(studying the bird)* Let's see . . . let's see . . . Scissors?

ILANA: Right over there.

> *He gets them.*

ANDY: Will you spot me?

ILANA: Yeah.

> *Andy climbs onto the couch and then onto the ottoman.*

ANDY: Don't let me fall.

ILANA: I won't.

> *Andy cuts the string and the bird falls.*

ANDY: *Yes! Big-time yes!*

> *He gets down. He puts the ottoman back. He picks up the bird.*

ANDY: Fan-freaking-tastic.

> *He looks at her. He smiles like a kid.*

ANDY: Thank you.

ILANA: It's fine. It's fine. It's . . .

ANDY: What?

ILANA: Nothing, I . . .
(forcing herself) Thank you for reading my book.

ANDY: I love your book! Thank you for writing it!

ILANA: Okay.

ANDY: Can I ask you something?

ILANA: Okay.

ANDY: How did you get the idea for it?

ILANA: I don't know. I just did.

ANDY: You "just did." *Wow. Wow.*

ILANA: I mean . . .
(beat) When I was thirteen, I had this sort of medallion of a dragonfly, it was made out of pieces of volcanic glass. It hung in my bedroom window and it was like my favorite thing.
But when my family moved, I lost it. I was so upset.
I was really . . . so upset.

I don't know, it was the first time I realized that things could just vanish from your life.

And then, I don't remember why, but one day I just started to fold it. I had a piece of paper, and I made this one single fold in it . . . I stared at it . . . and then I slowly started to . . . I don't know, I tried to fold my lost dragonfly. I tried to make the paper look like volcanic glass.

ANDY: Are you going to . . .

Um . . .

Are you going to fold your dog?

ILANA: *What?*

ANDY: Something you lost. Are you going to fold your lost dog?

ILANA: No.

No, that's . . .

You don't understand.

I think you should probably go.

ANDY: Oh. Okay. Okay, yeah, I should probably get going . . .

> *Andy starts to put on his shoes. He has to sit on the floor to do this. His laces are knotted and he has to work hard to untie them.*

ANDY: So . . . Do you ever . . .

Ha!

Do you ever . . . tutor people?

ILANA: What?

ANDY: Tutor. Origami.

ILANA: No. I don't ever do that.

ANDY: Of course not. But would you? I mean . . . *would* you?

ILANA: No. I never would. You seem very nice, but no.

ANDY: Oh, it's not for me! Silly Andy! I would never even *presume* that you'd tutor *me*! Gosh, sometimes I'm a *huge* idiot!

ILANA: Oh . . .

ANDY: I have this student . . .

ILANA: Oh. Right.

ANDY: Great kid! And he's big into folding, and . . .

ILANA: Yeah, I don't do that.

ANDY: Look, this kid. He was taking calculus as a freshman.

ILANA: I'm sure he's very talented.

ANDY: We have a calculus club. It's like an after-school activity for anyone who's into calc.

ILANA: Sounds wild.

ANDY: Suresh is his name. He shows up and he's the hit of the club. It wasn't just about calculus, it was about winding Suresh up and watching him run his mouth.

ILANA: He sounds like a great kid.

ANDY: Trust me. Suresh is tops.

ILANA: I just don't tutor. I'm not a people person, and I'm not a good teacher.

ANDY: You are though. Your class, your book . . . I mean, you kind of really affected me, you know? I don't say it lightly.

ILANA: Well, that's very . . .
That's not . . .
I don't tutor.

ANDY: That's too bad.
(beat) His mother died last year.

ILANA: Wow. How sad.

ANDY: She was crossing the street and she got hit by a car, and the car took off. A hit and run. They never caught the guy.

ILANA: You know, that's awful, but you're not going to guilt me into anything, okay? I don't feel guilt. I'm immune to guilt. I don't fucking tutor.

ANDY: I'm not! I'm sorry! I'm so sorry it came out that way.

ILANA: Origami doesn't need tutors. He can read books, he can go on the Internet, he can fold whatever he wants. There's nothing I could say that would make him any better or any worse.

ANDY: You won't tutor him. I get it.

ILANA: Send him over to MIT. They've got that origami club. They're all hotshots.

ANDY: I know all about the MIT origami club and you'll understand if I don't want to expose my student to that sort of collegiate hedonism.
Besides, you're the best there is.

ILANA: No, I'm not.

ANDY: Yes, you are.

ILANA: Is this why you came here today? To try and get me to tutor your student in origami?

ANDY: That's not the only reason I came. I just thought I'd try. I'm sorry.

ILANA: Okay. Fine. Now go.

> *Andy, still seated, still can't untie his shoes. But he grabs his bag and takes out a plastic shoe box. He opens it and slides it over to Ilana.*

ANDY: He's been doing origami for like three months. And those are some of his models.

> *Ilana looks into the box. She starts taking out beautiful origami models of insects and animals.*

ILANA: Your student folded these?

ANDY: There's a Moroccan hissing cockroach. Actual size. Physiologically accurate. One piece of paper.
There's a tarantula. Same thing.

ILANA: Wait . . . your . . . *student* folded *these?* He folded these himself? Did you show him how to do this?

ANDY: Are you kidding? *I* can't fold those.

Ilana, *Suresh sees folds before they happen.*

He looks at a flat piece of paper and sees everything that needs to be done. It's like he has X-ray vision.

> *Ilana pulls out an extremely complex geometric shape.*

ANDY: He did a bunch of animals and then became obsessed with complex polyhedra. Ilana, you've never seen someone fold like this kid. He's like Jimi Hendrix if Jimi Hendrix folded polyhedral origami.

ILANA: This doesn't make any sense.

ANDY: Why not?

ILANA: Because these . . .

ANDY: It's good, right?

ILANA: *(looks at him)*
It's really good.

ANDY: Listen: it's the middle of Suresh's junior year last year and his mother is killed by this hit and run. I mean, it's just awful. And poor Suresh, once he comes back to school, he's just . . . he's just a shell of the kid we knew. Which is understandable, but it was so hard to see him like that.

And then that summer he and his sister and his dad went to India. And when he came back to start his senior year, I mean, he just stopped caring or something.

He dropped out of Calc Club, which, you know, *that* hurt. Of course, he's still pulling straight As with his eyes closed. He had his pick of colleges and then he up and decides to go to *Brown.* He got in to *Yale and MIT* and he's going to *Brown.* I mean, this kid is acting up every which way.

He's in my advanced calc class and just sleeping through it. He's way ahead of everyone in there. This kid knows way more than me.

So I think to myself: I love this kid. I feel bad for him. Why waste that mind of his? So I gave him a book of basic folds.

> *Andy looks in the box and pulls out an origami toad.*

ANDY: Look at this. Look at this frog. He did this after about two weeks of folding in his whole life.

ILANA: He did this after two weeks?

ANDY: Two weeks. Most people start by folding a boat or a flower. He folds an Amazonian toad.

Ilana studies the model.

ANDY: I want to help him. And I thought . . .
He's just too smart for everyone else.
But he's not too smart for you.

ILANA: I don't know, I have to think. I'm sorry. I have to think about this.

ANDY: I totally understand!
(the models) Look, keep those. Hold on to them. I put my card in there. Call me. Think about it. And thanks for this bird.
Boy, I hope it stopped raining!

ILANA: Either way, you have to take that with you.

Andy puts out his hand to shake hers.

ANDY: Ilana, as always, it's been a pleasure.

They shake hands.

ILANA: Bye.

ANDY: So long!

He picks up the bird and plays with it, making hawk sounds.

ANDY: *Caw! Caw!*

He "flies" it out of the room, exiting.

ANDY: *(off stage) Caw! Caw!*

Ilana closes the door behind him. She goes to her couch. She looks at Suresh's models, marveling at them, touching them as if they were precious and delicate. She looks up to where the hawk had hung, and is now conscious of its absence.

She looks on her coffee table and sees that Andy forgot his little book.

ILANA: Great.

She looks at it. She flips through it.

She begins to read it. She becomes absorbed by it. Lights fade as hip-hop music fills the space . . .

Scene 2.

Ilana's studio. A few days later. The place is still a mess. Ilana is out of her robe, but still disheveled. She's still reading Andy's book. She's engrossed in it. She flips through it, finding other pages, as if trying to piece a story together.

The buzzer buzzes. Ilana, once again, is startled. She goes to the intercom.

ILANA: Hello?

SURESH: *(intercom)* Yo.

ILANA: *Hello?* Who is it?

SURESH: Yo.

ILANA: Suresh? Andy's student?

SURESH: What up?

ILANA: I thought you weren't supposed to come until noon.

SURESH: It's noon.

ILANA: It is?

SURESH: Yup. High noon.

> *Ilana takes her hand off the intercom.*

ILANA: Shit.

> *She buzzes him in.*
>
> *She puts Andy's book on the table and tries to straighten herself up.*
>
> *She opens the door. A few seconds later, Suresh enters.*
>
> *He's got his iPod earphones in his ears.*

ILANA: Hi. Sorry. I lost track of time. Suresh?

SURESH: Hey.

ILANA: I'm Ilana. Andy told me all about you.

SURESH: Who's Andy?

ILANA: Mr. Froling.

SURESH: Fro Dog.

ILANA: Yes, "Fro Dog." How are you?

SURESH: I'm cool.
What happened in here?

ILANA: What do you mean?

SURESH: I mean, what happened in here?

> *Ilana looks around.*

ILANA: Nothing.

SURESH: *Something . . .*

> *Beat.*

ILANA: Well come on in.

SURESH: You like some organic hip-hop?

ILANA: What?

SURESH: These some smooth cuts. Check it . . .

> *Suresh takes one of his earphones out of his ears and puts it into Ilana's ear. They're connected by his earphones. They stand very close to each other and he plays music that fills the space. He sways along with it, almost as if he's dancing with her.*
>
> *After a while, he removes the earphone from his ear and puts it in Ilana's other ear. The music swells. He sways off. He looks around her studio at origami models while Ilana stands there listening to music. She's taken aback by the whole thing.*
>
> *Suresh picks up Andy's book and starts flipping through it. Ilana rips the earphones out, the music stops.*

ILANA: Put that down!

SURESH: What's this?

ILANA: Put it down!

> *He does.*

ILANA: That's none of your business!

> *She picks up the book and holds it.*

SURESH: Okay. Sorry.

ILANA: Here.

> *She hands him back his iPod.*

SURESH: *(the music)* Dope, right?

ILANA: Fascinating. Thank you.

SURESH: What is that, your diary or something?

ILANA: No.

SURESH: What is it?

ILANA: Nothing. Just something I've been reading. Look, why don't we sit down and, you know, you can fold me something.

SURESH: Protective.

ILANA: What?

SURESH: Protective.

ILANA: What's protective?

SURESH: You arc. Of your reading material.
  This place is crazy.

ILANA: Yeah. It's crazy.

SURESH: Fro Dog said you were like a professional origami person.

ILANA: Yeah, I am.

SURESH: Could I get something to drink?

ILANA: Sure, I've got water, tea, and milk.

SURESH: What kind of milk?

ILANA: I don't know. Skim milk.

SURESH: Skim? Hell no. I don't drink no skim milk.
  Why you got all these hearts?

ILANA: I'm studying it.

SURESH: The heart?

ILANA: Yeah.

SURESH: Why?

ILANA: It's a job.

SURESH: Origami?

ILANA: Yeah.

SURESH: Someone paying you money to fold a heart?

ILANA: No.

SURESH: So why you folding a heart?

ILANA: It's a project.
I'm trying to fold a mesh heart sleeve.

SURESH: A mesh what?

ILANA: Heart. Sleeve.
It's a project commissioned by a medical research team. It's complicated.

SURESH: What, too complicated for a dumb kid like me?

ILANA: No.

SURESH: So?

ILANA: Okay, so in treating congestive heart failure, usually you need open heart surgery. It's invasive. You have to crack open a person's sternum.
Here: show me your fist.

> *Suresh holds out his fist.*

> *As she speaks, Ilana uses her own hand as the mesh heart and pantomimes it slowly unwrapping around Suresh's fist.*

ILANA: Okay, so your heart is about the size of your fist, right? So these doctors have developed a way to insert a small tube into a person's chest and, through that tube, pump in a mesh netting which, when it exits the tube, unfolds in such a way that it can surround the heart, providing pressure.

> *Her hand is wrapped around Suresh's fist.*

ILANA: It's a new treatment.

SURESH: That's tight.

ILANA: My job is to devise a crease pattern for this mesh netting so that it unfolds precisely around the heart.

SURESH: You gonna account for the heartbeat?

ILANA: Let's hope so.

SURESH: I mean, the heart is always pumping.

> *Suresh squeezes his fist and twists it in a hard
> rhythm, as if it were a beating heart.*

ILANA: Yes, the heart is always beating, and so we're talking about
some serious crease patterns.
It's a matter of predictability.

SURESH: Predictability how?

ILANA: *(she gets a piece of paper)* Well, for example, if I'm going to fold
this . . .

> *She almost folds the paper, but then stops.*

SURESH: Yeah? What?

ILANA: Nothing, look, why don't you fold something?

SURESH: No, but show me what you were going to show me.

ILANA: Later. I want to see you fold something.

SURESH: But how are you gonna do it?

ILANA: I'm going to figure it out.

SURESH: How?

ILANA: I just will.

SURESH: Word.

> *He holds his fist out for a fist bump.*

ILANA: What?

SURESH: Hit it. Come on, now. Fist bump.

> *She awkwardly fist bumps him.*

SURESH: That's what I'm talking about.
It's like our hearts bumping.
Heart bump.
Ba-dump, ba-dump.

> *He wanders around her apartment, looking at her models.*
>
> *He picks up a rabbit origami piece from a shelf.*

ILANA: So . . . Andy said you have like a senior project.

SURESH: Who's Andy?

ILANA: Fro Dog.

SURESH: Fro Dizzle.

ILANA: He said you might want to, you know, study origami. I guess. Although I really don't know what you'd want to do here.

SURESH: This place is crazy.

ILANA: Yeah. It's crazy.

SURESH: What is this, a rabbit?

ILANA: Yeah.

SURESH: It don't look like a rabbit.

ILANA: Well, it's a rabbit.

SURESH: It looks like a dog.

ILANA: It's a rabbit, okay?

SURESH: I could fold a better rabbit than this one.

ILANA: Then do it.

> *Suresh's phone rings. He checks it and then silences it.*

SURESH: All I'm saying is that if you gonna be designing a mesh heart to get pumped into someone's chest, you better work on your rabbits first.

ILANA: Thanks for the advice.

SURESH: Do you really think this rabbit is good?

ILANA: No, okay? That rabbit is not good. It's flawed. It lacks a rabbit essence. But we're not going to fold brilliant pieces of origami every time we sit down. We mess around with a model, we play with it, we test crease patterns, and after a few tries, if we're lucky, we come out with a model that satisfies our aesthetic standards. Okay? So, yeah, that rabbit sucks. So what? It's a sketching.

SURESH: Yeah, a sketching of a dog.

ILANA: *(frustrated)* It's not a dog, it's a rabbit!

> Suresh looks at her, and then goes back to studying
> the rabbit.

ILANA: You don't do sketchings, do you?

SURESH: Huh?

ILANA: You don't have to try and "figure out" a model. You just do it, isn't that right? You just see something and know how to fold it.

SURESH: I dunno.

ILANA: Look, I saw your models.

SURESH: The ones Fro Dog brought over?

ILANA: Yeah. These.

> Suresh shrugs.

SURESH: They're not that good.

ILANA: Yes, they are. You're very good.
  Will you fold something right now?

SURESH: I don't feel like it.

ILANA: Why are you even here?

SURESH: Fro Dog.

ILANA: Fro Dog *what*?

SURESH: He told me to come. He was really excited and everything, I guess that, you know . . .
  You're like his hero or something.
  He told me to come.
  Fro Dog's my boy, you know? So I come.

ILANA: What are you talking about?

SURESH: Fro Dog said your dog ran off.

ILANA: He told you that?

SURESH: Yeah, he was talking about it. He seemed real concerned about you and everything. Because of your divorce and that your dog ran off and you're living in this place and not answering your phone and all that.

ILANA: Okay, that's enough.
  Everyone knows a little too much about me these days.

SURESH: You check the pound? For the dog?

ILANA: Yes I checked the pound! I checked every pound every day for a month. Of course I checked the stupid pound.

SURESH: So where'd he go?

ILANA: I don't know.

SURESH: Usually you gotta keep a dog tied up.

ILANA: Oh my God . . . Look, my dog was twelve years old. He had three legs, no teeth, and no ears either. Wherever he ran off to, he's not alive anymore. Some animals, I guess they want to die alone.

SURESH: How come he didn't have any ears?

ILANA: His previous owner cut them off with hedge clippers.

SURESH: Why?

ILANA: I don't know, because his previous owner was an abusive piece of shit. He's going to rot in hell. You traumatize a dog, you rot in hell. Simple as that.

SURESH: What about a cat?

ILANA: Fuck cats. Look, are you going to fold something or not? Because if you don't want to be here, then just leave.

SURESH: You miss him?

ILANA: My dog?

SURESH: Yeah.

ILANA: What do you think?

SURESH: I guess you must miss him.

ILANA: I do.

SURESH: Fro Dog said you got a divorce because the dog ran off.

ILANA: Fro Dog talks too much.

SURESH: Word.

ILANA: Why do you talk like that?

SURESH: Talk like what?

ILANA: The way you speak. It's incongruous.

SURESH: I talk the way I talk.

ILANA: But you talk the way you talk for a reason.

SURESH: Why do *you* talk like *that*?

ILANA: I'm just asking.

SURESH: You think I should sound Indian or something?

ILANA: Not at all.

SURESH: Then how should I sound then?

ILANA: Any way you like.

SURESH: Okay, then, so this is how I like.

ILANA: Why don't you just cool it with the attitude?

SURESH: Why don't you just suck my dick?

ILANA: *Excuse me?!*

SURESH: Talking about, *why you talk black like that?* Racist.

ILANA: Fuck you.

SURESH: I don't have to talk any way I don't want to talk, bitch.

ILANA: Did you just call me a bitch?

SURESH: Yeah, bitch, I called you a bitch.

ILANA: *Get the fuck out of my studio!*

SURESH: Fine!

ILANA: Leave!

> *Suresh's phone starts ringing.*

SURESH: You gotta relax.

> *Phone still rings.*

ILANA: Just get out of here.

> *Phone rings. Suresh looks at it.*

SURESH: I gotta take this.

ILANA: Take it outside! I'm serious . . .

> *He answers it. Everything about his voice and manner changes. He turns away from Ilana, not wanting her to see or hear this.*

SURESH: Hi dad.
What's wro . . . ? Where's Rahel?
Dad, just . . .
(beat) Go into the freezer. There's some chicken in a Ziploc. Just take it out and put it in the sink.
(beat) I'm taking care of it, okay?
(beat) I know you're hungry. I know.
In the freezer.
The *sink.*

No nothing's going to happen, it's going to defrost.
I'm coming home now. We'll eat. Okay?
Okay. Bye dad.

He hangs up.

SURESH: I gotta go.

They look at each other.

SURESH: I'm sorry I told you to suck my dick. That shit is
disrespectful.

Ilana doesn't know what to say to him.

SURESH: I'm out.

He starts to leave.

ILANA: You cook?

SURESH: Huh?

ILANA: You're cooking dinner tonight?

SURESH: I cook dinner every night.
How many times you gonna have to sketch out that mesh heart
before it's ready?

ILANA: As many times as it takes.

SURESH: What if it doesn't work?

ILANA: I don't know. I hope it does.

SURESH: Yeah.
What's the medium anyway, some sort of synthetic fiber?

ILANA: Something like that.

SURESH: Shit. That's tough.
Pleats are gonna drive you crazy on this.

ILANA: Yeah. They are.

SURESH: You know what I learned the other day about pleats? You
know how the only way to get rid of a pleat is?

ILANA: You have to collide it with another pleat.

> *Suresh holds out his fist. Ilana awkwardly fist bumps him.*

SURESH: Word. Shit is wack.

Scene 3.

> *Lights shift. The doorbell rings. Ilana buzzes the buzzer.*

> *Moments later Andy enters.*

ANDY: Hey!

ILANA: Hey.

ANDY: Hey! Thanks for letting me come over again.
    What a flake I am! I've never forgotten that thing in my entire life. I'm kind of lost without it. How's it going? How did it go with Suresh? He seemed pretty excited about you.

ILANA: He did?

ANDY: Oh yeah! He's really excited to do his senior project here and everything. Your apprentice! The sorcerer's apprentice!

ILANA: He called me a bitch.

ANDY: He *what?*

ILANA: He told me to suck his dick.

ANDY: *What?*

ILANA: Other than that, nice kid. Quality kid.

ANDY: I am *so sorry.* I had no idea! Oh Suresh!

ILANA: He came all the way over here, and he wouldn't fold anything. He doesn't even *like* folding. He said he came over here as a favor for you.

ANDY: He said that? A favor for *me*? He was so excited in class today! He said you were amazing and everything!

ILANA: He's a real piece of work.

ANDY: *(remembers something in his bag)* Oh, and he wanted me to give you this!

> *Andy takes out a small origami rabbit.*

ANDY: It's a rabbit! He folded it for you!

> *Ilana takes it and looks at it.*

ILANA: I hate this kid.

ANDY: No! He's a great kid! Trust me! He wanted me to tell you to unfold it.
He said there's a message inside.

ILANA: Yeah, I bet there is, the little brat.

> *But she starts to unfold the model carefully.*

ANDY: So . . . um . . . my book?

ILANA: It's right there.

> *Andy sees his book and takes it.*

ANDY: Great! I guess I was so excited to get that hawk. Great hawk, by the way. It's in the den! I have a little room, I call it the den. It's where I fold.

> *Ilana unfolds the rabbit. Suresh has written a note on the paper. She reads it.*

ANDY: What's it say?

> *Ilana reads it carefully again.*

ILANA: I don't know. It's like a poem or something. A poem in a rabbit.

ANDY: See? Great kid.

ILANA: What is it with you guys?
I've got Suresh writing me poems and I've got you writing about my book and my scaled koi and the stupid dress I wore at the convention last summer.

ANDY: What?

ILANA: Your blessings. Your counted blessings.

ANDY: Your dress? I didn't read you that one. That one about your dress.

Ilana looks at Andy.

ILANA: Right . . .

ANDY: Did you read this?

ILANA: Your book? Well, I . . . I mean . . .

ANDY: You read my book?!

ILANA: You left it here!

ANDY: You *read* this!?
You don't just *read* somebody's *book*!

ILANA: I read it, Andy, but can you just listen to me . . .

ANDY: It's *private*! It's a very private thing!

ILANA: You took it out. You read to me from it.

ANDY: Select entries!

ILANA: It was just sitting there, and I picked it up and I, you know, I started flipping through it . . .

ANDY: You might have gotten the *idea* that these things might be *slightly personal*. You might have stopped reading.
I mean, there's other stuff in here . . .

ILANA: I shouldn't have read it. Andy, I shouldn't have read it, I'm sorry. But I started and I couldn't put it down.

Andy paces around and then stops.

ANDY: Look, for a long time, Ilana . . . I've really . . .

I took your class on the scaled koi last summer at the convention and you were wearing this green dress. This green summer dress. And that's why I couldn't fold the koi. I was just watching you fold and talk and walk around and . . .

I really like you. I mean, I have a really big crush on you.

ILANA: I know, it was in the book.

ANDY: Oh *man!*

ILANA: Andy, listen . . .

ANDY: People have two sides, okay? They have their inside and their outside, and I don't really need for everyone to be reading my book! Nobody's ever read this before.

ILANA: People have more than two sides.

ANDY: Some people. But not me. There's this. And then there's *this.*

ILANA: But *this . . . this* is . . .

ANDY: What?

ILANA: It's amazing, Andy.

ANDY: No it's not.

ILANA: It is. It's just so . . . *Weird . . .*

ANDY: Yeah, great.

ILANA: But it was, I mean, I have to tell you . . . it was creepy seeing myself in there. It felt invasive.

ANDY: Well I'm *sorry!* I didn't mean for you to read it!

ILANA: But it was more than that. There's so much in there and I've been trying to figure it out. I mean, it's like a catalog of everything that's ever happened to you . . . even your wisdom teeth, even mosquito bites, even your . . . your . . . *wisdom teeth!*

ANDY: How much of this did you *read?*

ILANA: I read all of it.

ANDY: Oh jeez!

I have to go.

He turns to go.

ILANA: Don't go . . .

ANDY: Now you know everything I might have told you, anything I might ever have told you . . . you know it all now, so it's been nice knowing you. Thank you. Good-bye.

ILANA: *(a little desperate)* Please don't go . . .

He stops and looks at her.

ILANA: Don't leave. Just stay for a second?
I mean . . . You come barging in here and you take my hawk and you leave your blessings and, you know, it would be great if you just didn't leave for a second. Could you just not leave for a second?

Andy turns as if he might stay a little bit longer.

An awkward silence.

ANDY: I had seven wisdom teeth.
My X-rays are in textbooks for oral surgeons.
So I'm kind of famous.

ILANA: Yeah. Yeah, I know, I read it.

ANDY: Right.

Awkward silence.

ANDY: What was Suresh's poem about?

ILANA: It was about my dog.

ANDY: Oh, that's nice. That's a nice thing for a poem.

ILANA: You need to tell me something. I read your book. I read it twice, Andy. There's something you need to tell me.

ANDY: Okay . . .

ILANA: You always write . . . as one of your "blessings" . . . you always write, "I've never been hurt."

ANDY: So?

ILANA: You write it about twenty-five times or more throughout the book. "I've never been hurt. Not really."

ANDY: I haven't.

ILANA: And then, you know, this book is just filled with . . .
It's filled with *pain*, all these really awful and tough things that have happened to you.
I mean, your parents.
Your sister.
The time you tried stand-up comedy.

ANDY: I *really* wish you hadn't read this.

ILANA: So can you just tell me how you can be thankful for these things?

ANDY: I don't know.

ILANA: I mean, what is a blessing anyhow? Anything? Can it be anything?

ANDY: I don't know what they are, they're my feelings. I think about them and I write them down. It's just what I do. And I have been hurt once. I hurt my elbow.

ILANA: Pain isn't a blessing. Unless you're totally crazy, it's not something you sit around being thankful for. It just isn't.

ANDY: I don't know. It might be.
It's not *pleasant* . . . but it's real.
Anyhow, it's just my book. It's just stuff I write.
I don't expect you to understand.
Nobody understands me.

> *Ilana cautiously goes to him and kisses him. She steps away.*

ANDY: Okay. Wow.

He steps toward her. Nervously leans in and kisses her longer.

Lights shift and hip-hop music fills the air. Suresh enters and begins cleaning the space. Eventually Andy and Ilana exit.

Scene 4.

Ilana's studio, one month later. The studio is immaculately organized and clean.

Suresh, with iPod earbuds in his ears, at a table, folding a fourteen-inch tyrannosaurus.

Ilana enters with a stack of mail. She's well dressed and groomed for the first time, coming from a business meeting. She stops and looks at the studio, seeing it organized and clean for the first time.

She's not happy about it. She yells Suresh's name, but he can't hear her until the third time she yells . . .

ILANA: *Suresh!*

Suresh takes out his earbuds, the music stops.

SURESH: Yo, what up?

ILANA: What happened here!?

SURESH: What?

ILANA: What did you *do* to this place?

SURESH: I cleaned it.

ILANA: What did you do with all my things?

SURESH: I threw 'em out.

ILANA: *What?!*

SURESH: Chill! I'm kidding! I put it in boxes and stacked them in the closet. And I put your documents and shit in the file cabinet. And over there I got some crates filled with your folding paper. It's a lot more efficient this way.

ILANA: This is not what I asked you to do.

SURESH: I asked you if I could straighten up.

ILANA: "Straighten up!"

SURESH: Check it out: shit is straightened.

ILANA: You can't come into my home and change everything!

SURESH: Why you gotta always be like this?

ILANA: I thought you were just going to throw away the food!

SURESH: You know, I got on my knees and scrubbed the damn kitchen floor. There was some nasty shit all in that grout, you know? I even got behind the fridge.

ILANA: Where's my crease patterns?

SURESH: In the box marked "crease patterns."

> *Ilana goes to a stack of boxes. Suresh puts the earphones back in. Hip-hop fills the air. Ilana starts speaking again, but we can't hear her.*

> *She realizes Suresh can't hear her. She shouts his name again.*

ILANA: *Suresh!*

> *He takes the earphones out, music out.*

SURESH: *What?*

ILANA: Can you turn off your music for two seconds? Where's . . . where's that . . . um . . . there was an envelope . . . it was marked I think with . . .

SURESH: The mesh heart shit?

ILANA: No. Yeah, I mean . . . the documents from the medical team.

SURESH: File cabinet. Top drawer.

Ilana goes to it.

SURESH: So how'd it go?

ILANA: It went fine.

SURESH: They cool with you?

ILANA: It went fine.

SURESH: What did you tell them?

ILANA: Listen to your music.

SURESH: I don't want to anymore.

ILANA: Fine.

SURESH: Fine.

ILANA: It's going to blizzard. You should probably get home. It's going to dump on us tonight.

Ilana goes to the fridge and takes out a carton of milk, which she drinks from for the rest of the scene.

SURESH: A tempestuous Valentine's Day. Fro Dog taking you out?

ILANA: Huh? Yeah, sure.

SURESH: Frodesiac! Candlelight dinner and everything.

Ilana suddenly looks around for something.

ILANA: Suresh, where's the fire extinguisher?

SURESH: Where's the fire?

She finds the fire extinguisher and puts it on the kitchen counter and holds it for a moment, relieved.

ILANA: What is that, a dinosaur?

SURESH: Word. A tyrannosaurus. I love the tyrannosaurus.

Anybody who says they have another favorite dinosaur is *lying*. Trust me. You can't love dinosaurs and not be like BFF with the T. rex. You know what I'm saying?

ILANA: Whatever. I like the brontosaurus. That's my favorite.

SURESH: That's cause you're a woman. Brontosaurus is a woman's dinosaur.

ILANA: So? tyrannosaurus is juvenile.

SURESH: Shut up.

ILANA: *You* shut up.

> *Ilana flops on the couch.*

ILANA: I can't work in a clean environment. It's just the way I am. I need to see everything at once. I need clutter.

SURESH: Clutter'll grow back.

> *Suresh gets a plastic shoe box.*

SURESH: I folded something for you, it might be helpful for the mesh heart . . .

ILANA: Jesus, how much did you fold today?

SURESH: The T. rex.

But I finished some other stuff I've been working on, too.

I busted a phat icosahedron using that Japanese stone tile #14 with the foil-looking backside. That shit is off the hook. And then *this*, though . . . this is some serious action . . .

ILANA: *(half-laughing, half-serious)* Would you just stop!

SURESH: What?

ILANA: Just stop!

SURESH: Okay . . .

ILANA: I just need you to slow down. Do you understand? I mean, I come home and my whole place has just *morphed* into somebody else's space and I'm trying to just gather my thoughts and you're here folding away. Just folding away.

SURESH: I thought I was supposed to.

ILANA: Could you stop being a genius for two minutes please? Listen to your music.

SURESH: *You* should listen to my music! Don't you have a stereo or something?

ILANA: My ex took the stereo. He took all the music.

SURESH: You want, I can burn you some CDs.

ILANA: What? Rap music?

SURESH: Hip-hop.

ILANA: No thank you.

SURESH: You haven't even listened to it.

ILANA: I don't need to listen to something to know I'm not going to like it.

SURESH: How can you even say that? Of course you do. Especially you.

ILANA: Why especially me?

SURESH: You been struggling with that mesh heart? Why? Because you haven't found the zone yet.

ILANA: I'm not struggling.

SURESH: I'm just saying, music can help. When Fro Dog gave me those books, I cruised through the animals and shit real fast. It was the complex polyhedra that threw me for the loop. So I'm sitting there, trying to wrap my brain around that shit, and I got my iPod on, you know? And I'm listening to this MC laying down these dope rhymes, freestyling, and there was something about his rhymes and his voice that just sort of spoke to my paper, to my hands. So I always think that folding is just like freestyling. It's like folding is like the evolution of a rhyme. So you gotta freestyle a little bit.

ILANA: I gotta freestyle. Thanks for the advice.

SURESH: Yeah, improvising your rhymes. Or your folds.
Like, say you want to fold a simple cube. Boring. Okay, but here's where you start, a simple fold, a simple rhyme. So I'm gonna freestyle. On what? What should I rap about?

ILANA: What, you're going to rap?

SURESH: Yeah, give me a topic.

ILANA: Anything?

SURESH: Yeah, give me something.

ILANA: Okay . . . um . . .
(she holds up her carton of milk) Okay, how about milk?

SURESH: Milk.

ILANA: Yeah. Rap about milk.

SURESH: That's wack.

ILANA: Well, that's what I want.

SURESH: Awright. Shit.
Okay. What is that? Nasty-ass skim milk?

ILANA: That's exactly what it is.

SURESH: Skim.
Awright then.
Check it:
One percent, two percent, skim, and whole
Drink it down fast, make your body feel cold
Keep your bones strong now, even when you're old
May not want to do it, but you'll do what you're told.
Okay, right?

ILANA: *(sarcastic)* Very impressive.

SURESH: But that's simple. I figure, we take it to the next level. If that was a cube, let's say this next rhyme is like, an octahedron.
(he thinks) See, I'm all about prevention of osteoporosis
But some motherfuckers gonna always oppose this

With bones so bad you got halitosis
And they splinter and crack and I know that you know this.

ILANA: Yeah, it's cute, Suresh. I'm glad you can rhyme about milk. Somehow I don't see this helping me fold the mesh heart.

SURESH: But check it: it's still too simplistic. It's a basic rhyme scheme. The rhyme always comes on the last word.

It's like if you had all your folds in the same place? You'd never fold anything cool.

So the adept MCs they'll fold their rhymes in different places. And so the shape of their language is unpredictable. Unpredictability! It's a good thing . . . in music, in origami.

ILANA: Do you even read music?

SURESH: What, like notes and shit on a page?

ILANA: Yeah, notes on a page.

SURESH: Hell no.

ILANA: I figured you didn't. Rap has no musical notation. There's no way of writing it down.

SURESH: Why's music gotta be written down? You gotta just play it, sing it, freestyle it. Like this: check it—

ILANA: Great. More milk rhymes.

SURESH: I'm trying to demonstrate something to you, okay? Why you gotta be so mean about it?

ILANA: Okay okay okay . . .

SURESH: I'm about to up the ante. We about to fold a stellated truncated icosahedron.

I'm gonna bust some serious shit now, Ilana. You ready for some serious shit?

ILANA: I am ready for some serious shit.

SURESH: *(he bobs his head, thinking; this is done slowly, with a tinge of uncertainty, since he is making it up as he goes along)*
My girl Ilana she don't know but she a lady madonna
She drinkin skim milk and dairy cause the calcium gonna

Give her bones and her tones and whatever she wanna
Cause she my prima Ilana
Homogenized her momma,
Supersized mañana
Hypothesized McDonald's fries
Would sweat her like a sauna.
Now the silk trade's gone
And the milkmaid's song
Can't be Kelis cause her milk shake kicked it back to Hong Kong.
My White Russian she's a lush and barely wearin a thong
She barely carryin along
A fairy tale that's gone wrong
She pullin tubes with ice cubes
Milky hits from the bong.

ILANA: *(laughs)* So you just made that up? Just now?

SURESH: Yeah, that was just off the top of my dome.

ILANA: You just invented those rhymes as you were speaking them?

SURESH: Word. And there's themes in there, you know, milkish themes. And if that were a crease pattern, it'd be all the fuck over the place.

ILANA: But it's not a crease pattern, it's a rhyme scheme.

SURESH: Same thing!

ILANA: No, not the same thing! And you can't freestyle something that's going to wrap around somebody's heart.

SURESH: Why not?

ILANA: Because it's too important.
It's somebody's sick heart. I'm not going to just wing it.
(beat) Just because you can fold anything you want doesn't mean you understand everything. You told me to think about tessellations. So I did. And it sounds good, but it really doesn't help at all. You might as well tell me to think about "shapes."
For me it's not about improvisation, it's about rigor, okay? If origami is music, it's a fugue. It's a repeating theme, painstakingly arranged on paper before you can do anything with it.

SURESH: *(dismissive; like a child)* You're a fugue.

ILANA: I am not a fugue.

SURESH: Yeah you are. You're just a repeating theme, sitting on your couch, eating the same damn Szechuan beef every night, complaining about everything and never folding nothing.

ILANA: Fuck you.

SURESH: And dropping F-bombs like mad.

ILANA: At least I can read music.

SURESH: So?

ILANA: You only understand things one way. You don't understand how I fold like I do.

SURESH: How do you fold then?

ILANA: So, look I have this one crease pattern . . . oh, you'd love this . . .

> *Ilana goes to look for it.*

ILANA: I had this terrific paper I bought in bulk from Japan, really strong, fibrous stuff, and I took it to this research and development company. I got permission to use their industrial laser cutter so I could make these complicated folds.

SURESH: You used a laser?

ILANA: It was cool.

SURESH: You used a laser to fold?

ILANA: If you put it on a really low setting, you can just score the paper. It's perfect for folding. You're gonna *love* this.

> *She can't find the stuff. Her files are all organized and put away.*

SURESH: It's kind of like cheating, though, right?

ILANA: It's not cheating.

SURESH: Cheating. Cheater. Laser-cheater.

ILANA: If I could even find my stuff maybe I could fucking show you.

SURESH: F-bomb. Cheater.

> *Ilana takes a large crate that Suresh had organized and dumps it on the floor. Paper everywhere.*

ILANA: Now I'll find it!

> *Suresh flips out, but Ilana doesn't realize how serious he is right away.*

SURESH: What are you doing!?

ILANA: I'm finding my stuff!

SURESH: I just did that! That took me all day!

ILANA: That's why I don't clean! It's a futile endeavor.

SURESH: *What's your problem!?*

ILANA: What?!

> *Suresh goes and tries to reorganize the paper.*

SURESH: It took me all day! I had everything in there totally organized, a whole system and . . . and why'd you go do this!

ILANA: Suresh! Calm down!

SURESH: *(realizing his organization is lost)* Aw shit, man! This is *fucked!* You fucked it all up!

ILANA: It's okay! It's just paper!

> *Suresh hits the ground and then gets up, facing her.*

SURESH: All that work and you just ruined it!

ILANA: *(slightly losing temper)* I didn't ask you to clean, Suresh, and it's just paper anyhow!

SURESH: This place was disgusting. Trash everywhere, junk everywhere.

That's probably why your husband left you. That's probably why your stupid dog ran off. Cause you're such a mess all the time.

> *Ilana steps back, hurt, far more than Suresh intended. She doesn't say or do anything, but it's clear to Suresh he hurt her.*

> *A long silence. Suresh wants to say something, to apologize but he doesn't know how. Somehow in this silence they agree to let it pass.*

ILANA: *(quietly)* You need to go home now. It's late, and it's going to blizzard.

> *Suresh gets his coat and bag.*

> *He goes to the plastic shoe box he had earlier. He opens it and takes out an origami three-dimensional life-sized human heart.*

SURESH: I made you a heart.

> *He gives it to her.*

> *Ilana takes it.*

SURESH: To help you with the mesh heart sleeve.

ILANA: When did you do this?

SURESH: I dunno. All week.
Everything's there. Every chamber and valve.
Exact proportions of an adult-sized human heart. Or mine, anyway. I made it the size of my fist.
Happy Valentine's Day or whatever.

> *Ilana holds the heart, amazed at its quality.*

ILANA: How did you do this?

> *Suresh looks at her, shakes his head.*

SURESH: *(points to a diagram of the heart)* I looked at that. And I folded it.

ACT 2
Scene 1.

> *A romantic restaurant, later that night. Ilana and Andy sit at a table sipping wine. Valentine heart décor surrounds them.*

ANDY: Valentine's Day! What a messed-up holiday.
I haven't had a date on Valentine's Day since . . . well . . . let's just say, it's been a long while.

ILANA: Since Maxine?

ANDY: *(chokes on his wine)* How do you know about Maxine?

ILANA: Your book, Andy.

ANDY: Oh for crying out loud.

ILANA: I'm sorry.

ANDY: Yes. Since Maxine.

ILANA: I should just . . . not mention it.

ANDY: Maxine and I . . . well, it wasn't the best relationship ever.

ILANA: I know.

ANDY: It was probably my worst relationship ever.

ILANA: Well . . . I mean, it was your only one, right?

ANDY: Jeez!

ILANA: I'm sorry. It's wrong of me to . . . I should just erase all that from my mind.

ANDY: Maxine.
Maximum Maxine.
Deep inside, a good person.

ILANA: I mean, she killed all your plants. On purpose.

ANDY: It's weird to not be able to lie a little to someone. I mean, you know? You know every detail about me now. Why should I even lie?

ILANA: Don't lie, then.

ANDY: I guess I'm going to try not to.
My heart. On a sleeve. For you.
(goes into his breast pocket) Which reminds me. Here.

> *From his breast pocket, Andy takes out a one-dimensional origami pink symmetrical heart valentine.*

ANDY: I made you a valentine.

ILANA: You did?

ANDY: I folded it.

ILANA: It's lovely!

ANDY: It's stupid.

ILANA: It's a lovely heart.

ANDY: It's a valentine.

ILANA: Andy . . . It's so sweet.

ANDY: Happy Valentine's Day.

ILANA: I didn't get you anything.

ANDY: Oh, don't worry about that.

ILANA: I just . . . I don't know, I've never been a huge fan of Valentine's Day.

ANDY: No, I know. I mean, it's a total corporate . . . commercial . . . consumer . . . event.

ILANA: Yeah. No. I mean, that's not why . . . I mean . . . about ten years ago . . . My husband and I, we were engaged at the time . . . I'm sorry. You probably don't want to hear this . . .

ANDY: No, I do!

ILANA: This is a . . . this is a pretty miserable story, but we were living in this tiny old house. This wasn't *on* Valentine's Day, it was like a week before, I think. And we both got really drunk and got into a huge argument. And Demba . . . Demba was our dog . . .

ANDY: The dog who ran off?

ILANA: Yeah, but this was when he was only about two years old . . . Demba would get really excitable, especially when Mike and I would fight. So we stuck Demba in the garage that night, because he kept barking and jumping around. You know, he was a shepherd mix . . . a big dog . . . anyhow, we were drunk and we passed out in separate rooms, and Mike passed out with a stupid cigarette in his hand. And the house caught fire, and neither of us woke up.

ANDY: Oh my God . . .

ILANA: See, the house was a mess anyway . . . but I had so much paper. Reams and reams of different paper, all over the place, hanging off the kitchen table, the sofa, all over the place. It went up quick. But Demba smelled the smoke, and he chewed his way through the door into the house. The door was solid . . . a really strong, hard wood. And he broke off most of his teeth, he got splinters in his gums . . . and he tore his way into our burning house and woke me up and then woke Mike up. And we got out. And the house burned down.

ANDY: That's incredible.

ILANA: So, Valentine's Day kind of always reminds me of being in the vet's office, while Demba had splinters removed from his gums.

ANDY: God!

> *They sip their wine. Ilana looks at Andy's valentine.*

ANDY: He was a good dog.

ILANA: Yeah he was.
He sure was.
Anyhow. Enough of that. Sorry. Not a great . . . I'm not the greatest date in the world tonight.

ANDY: You're perfect.

They smile at each other.

ILANA: Yeah. Perfecto.
(beat) Anyhow, in the mail today, I received an invitation. To a very exclusive origami convention.

ANDY: Really? Where?

ILANA: Nagasaki.

ANDY: Nagasaki?! Nagasaki, Japan?

ILANA: Some people I met back in the nineties. During the Bug Wars. Some of the best folders in Japan.

ANDY: Yeah!

ILANA: But it's really soon. Next month.

ANDY: Are you going to go?

ILANA: Oh, absolutely. And the interesting thing is, I can bring a guest.

ANDY: *Really?!*

ILANA: Yes, they'll provide room and board for a guest . . .

ANDY: Ilana! *Wow!* I mean . . . That's . . . so . . . I've never even been out of the country before!

ILANA: I was thinking about taking Suresh.

ANDY: Oh. Oh yeah, you should definitely take Suresh.

ILANA: I mean, he's my apprentice now. He's doing his senior project with me. I should take him.

ANDY: Of course.

ILANA: Andy, I'm sorry. I just thought—

ANDY: No! Jeez! Silly Andy!
Sometimes I just get ahead of myself.

Andy picks up another piece of bread. Lifts it to his

mouth, but then puts it down. He's trying not to show his disappointment.

ILANA: It's not that I wouldn't *want* you to come . . .

ANDY: No! I mean, of course.

ILANA: It would be a really great experience for Suresh. He'll see some things he's never seen before.

ANDY: Yeah. It would be great for him to see that, too. Those things.

ILANA: I think it's best. Don't you think?

ANDY: Of course. Absolutely of course.
Nagasaki!
(raises his glass) Here's to Nagasaki.

Ilana raises her glass.

ILANA: Here's to you, Fro Dog.

Andy laughs. They drink. Andy finishes his glass in a huge gulp. He pours another glass.

ANDY: Suresh's been calling me that since his freshman year.
Everyone at school calls me Fro Dog now.
All my life, I've never been cool.
But I'm a little cool now.
Suresh made me a little cool.
I mean, I'm not *really* cool. But I'm Fro Dog. "Fro Dog" is a thousand times cooler than "Mr. Froling."

ILANA: I think you're cool.

ANDY: No, you don't.
But it's okay, I don't mind.
(quotes) "So much of what I am is what I've lost."

ILANA: *(not registering)*
Mm-hm.

ANDY: I love that.

ILANA: Yeah.
What?

ANDY: That's you. That's from your book! "So much of what I am is what I've lost." I *love* that!

ILANA: Oh . . . oh yeah!

ANDY: You're amazing, you know that?

ILANA: *(quietly)* Yeah.
I mean.
Yeah, right.
Why do you like that book so much?

ANDY: What are you talking about? It's my favorite book!

ILANA: But it's not like . . . *literature*. It's not something you read for *wisdom*.

ANDY: I do.

ILANA: Andy, I'm not a writer, okay? I'm not a writer, I'm an origamist.

ANDY: But your essays . . .

ILANA: You're probably the only person who's ever bought it, much less read it, much less memorized it.

ANDY: Well, it *is* the number-two best-selling origami book in the country.

ILANA: Number two, huh?

ANDY: But it's one of a kind.

ILANA: My ex-husband . . . he copyedited my book. He really, really copyedited it.

ANDY: He did? Okay. So?

ILANA: The ideas were all mine. But I wrote some notes on each one, and then Mike, he, well . . . he wrote it out. I mean . . . those words you've memorized . . . those aren't my words. Those are Mike's words.

ANDY: Well, that's surprising.

ILANA: I wasn't trying to deceive anyone.

ANDY: It's still your book. It's still the things you lost. Why they're important to you. They're still your memories. And so it's still you.

ILANA: You read my book, I read yours. Yours is totally true, mine is ghostwritten. I know everything about you and you still don't know anything about me.

ANDY: So tell me something.

> *Ilana thinks.*

ILANA: Okay.
Okay, so . . .
I haven't folded a piece of paper since Demba ran away.

ANDY: You haven't? Why not?

ILANA: I don't know. I just can't do it anymore.

ANDY: But you're the best folder ever.

ILANA: No I'm not.

ANDY: So can't you fold now? Can you fold this napkin?

ILANA: No, I can't.

ANDY: Try. Just one fold. One fold to start.

ILANA: No, please, I can't.

> *Awkward beat. They both drink their wine.*

ANDY: Look, I know you read my book, so there's not a whole lot of mystery that I'm bringing to the table here? But I just want you to know something, and I'm speaking right now as a guy who's not himself, and as a guy who does not normally drink wine and is now on glass three: I think there's a good chance that I could be somebody very good for you. I think I could be the guy who comes into your life and helps you put it back together.

I am sitting right here, and I am a guy who will do anything for you, anything.

ILANA: That's very sweet.

ANDY: "Very sweet"?
That's the best I got, Ilana. I can't do better than that.

ILANA: I'm sorry.
I'm just . . .
(re: the chandeliered hearts) Look at these stupid hearts.
I hate Valentine's Day.
I'm a horrible person for this day.
I'm probably the wrong person you should be with.

ANDY: Ilana . . .
You're not, um . . . You not breaking up with me, are you?

ILANA: I don't know.

ANDY: Because it's Valentine's Day, and that would really suck.

She smiles at him.

ANDY: I'm trying to be more brave and impulsive. You make me want
to be that way.

ILANA: It's good to be brave and impulsive.

ANDY: Okay, then . . .
. . . Marry me.

ILANA: *What?*

ANDY: I swear to God, marry me. I know this is like our third date,
but I would marry you right now. Seriously. Brave and impulsive. Brave
and impulsive. Ilana, marry me.

ILANA: Andy, you need to stop drinking wine.

ANDY: This isn't the wine. Look, I know it's crazy, but what the heck.
Life is short, opportunities are scarce, love is rare. Marry me.

ILANA: You're serious.

ANDY: I'm serious.

ILANA: I'm not even divorced yet.

ANDY: Okay.

ILANA: So I can't marry you right now.

ANDY: But that's not a no.

ILANA: It's not a no. It's just reality.

ANDY: That's good. I'll take not a no. I'll take it.

> *She smiles at him and kisses him.*

ILANA: Nicest guy ever.
  (beat) I have to pee.

> *She exits. Andy looks after her, takes out his book, writes in it.*

Scene 2.

> *A hotel room in Nagasaki. Night. Suresh stands by a window, listening to his iPod/iPhone. We can hear his hip-hop. His cell rings, and he switches the music off and answers.*

SURESH: Yeah.
  Hey.
  Yeah, I'm here.
  How's dad?
  He did?
  Well what did you do?
  Why not?
  Rahel, what's your problem? I ask you to take care of one thing for one week and you . . .
  No, you shut up. How difficult is this? Huh?
  Hang up then! Fine, hang up then! What?

> *A knock at the door. Suresh goes to it, opens it, and walks away. Ilana enters.*

SURESH: *(still on phone)* No. I put everything in stupid Tupperware in the freezer and all you have to do is . . .

Well then do it then!

Forget it, I'm going. I hope you both starve.

Hello?

Hello?

Suresh hangs up and sits on the bed.

ILANA: *(concerned)* Are you okay?

SURESH: Me? Yeah, I'm cool. My stupid sister can't take control of the house for one week, is all.

ILANA: Where have you been?

SURESH: I been laying low.

ILANA: What happened to you today?

SURESH: Nothing happened.

ILANA: Where'd you go?

SURESH: Nowhere. I was in the garden.

ILANA: You missed the award ceremony. They gave you an award, but you weren't there.

SURESH: I didn't feel like going. What's your problem?

ILANA: I've been looking for you *all day*! You scared me.

I just didn't know where you were.

What were you doing in the garden?

SURESH: I was looking at the fish.

ILANA: You were looking at fish.

SURESH: Yeah.

ILANA: The whole day, looking at fish.

SURESH: I just felt like it, okay?

ILANA: Is this because of what happened this morning? At the memorial?

SURESH: Nothing happened at the memorial.

ILANA: You made that man cry.

SURESH: No I didn't.

ILANA: Yes you did.

SURESH: No I *did not.*

> *Suresh goes to the window.*
>
> *Ilana goes up to him. She touches his back. He recoils, as if she burned him.*

SURESH: *Whoa!* What! Don't touch me, okay?!

ILANA: Okay! I'm sorry! I only . . . I'm sorry, I'm sorry, okay?

SURESH: What do you want? I just want to . . . just don't do that.

ILANA: Suresh, I'm sorry.

SURESH: Yeah. Just . . .

ILANA: I'm sorry I touched you.

> *Suresh sits on the bed. And then he looks at Ilana.*

SURESH: I didn't mean to do that.
You can touch my back. I'm not a freak.

ILANA: No. You're not. I'm sorry.
Can I sit down here?

SURESH: Yeah.

> *She does. They're quiet for a moment.*

ILANA: You spent all day at the fish pond?

SURESH: Pretty much.

ILANA: What were the fish like?

SURESH: They would get into these feeding frenzies. I had pellets.

ILANA: You were feeding them?

SURESH: Big orange and white fish. Koi fish.
I never seen so many fishlike that.
I'm all about the fish pond.
(beat) You think when it happened, all the fish died too? I was wondering that when I was looking at the fish pond. You think they all died?

ILANA: I guess they must have.

SURESH: I mean, it was radioactive fire, right? Everywhere. But if they were deep down enough . . . they would have been okay, right?

ILANA: I don't know how deep you have to go to avoid something like that.

SURESH: Me neither. But I bet you could go deep enough. The smart fish probably did. There were some big old dudes swimming in there today. They would just chill, let the pellets come to them.
I loved those fish, you know?
They're like rolling around in the water, jumping on each other, feeding, feeding . . . It was like a rumble of activity, and the water's all green.

ILANA: It sounds nice.

SURESH: The fish went away after I ran out of pellets and it got dark. But I could see the moon in the water and everything.
I can see why people have fish ponds.
I can see why people look at fish.

ILANA: It seemed like you were . . . I don't know . . . *disturbed* this morning. I mean, the memorial. You didn't even speak after we left it.

SURESH: It's supposed to be disturbing.

ILANA: But what you did there . . . You understand why people were staring at you, and why, you know, that old man . . . how what you did made that man cry today, and how . . .

SURESH: *(suddenly angry)* I didn't make him cry.
(calms immediately) It's an emotional place. The place makes people cry.

ILANA: What you did there, what you folded.

SURESH: I was just folding.

ILANA: No you weren't.
You weren't just folding. Tell me why you folded those ravens.

SURESH: They weren't ravens, they were crows. Or blackbirds.
It didn't mean anything. It was just something different than all those stupid little paper doves.

ILANA: It meant something.

SURESH: No it didn't.

ILANA: Yes it does. Yes it does, see, you have this intense vision but you don't understand why you're folding what you are.
How you made their heads. The way their heads turned away.

SURESH: It's better to give a bird something to do.

ILANA: It meant something. You wouldn't have done it if it didn't mean anything.

SURESH: For you.

ILANA: Yes, for me. For that man. For everyone who was there watching you fold those birds and not speaking, not saying anything. When you fold paper, Suresh, people watch. They can't take their eyes off of you. And then when you fold something like those birds . . . it touches people.

SURESH: You're so stupid.

ILANA: Why? Why am I so stupid?

SURESH: Kids fold doves. They go there at the epicenter and fold doves. For *peace.* Or whatever.

ILANA: Yeah. And you unfolded them and folded these ravens.

SURESH: So, they've already been folded as something else, they have weird creases in wrong places. It gives them a wrinkled texture. They look old or something.

ILANA: They looked more than old. They looked . . . distraught. They looked heartbroken.

SURESH: *(angry)* They looked hungry, okay? Not distraught, not sad, just fucking hungry.

ILANA: Okay okay . . .

SURESH: I tried to fold the stupid things to make them look hungry.

ILANA: Why?

SURESH: I don't know why! Because the birds have nothing to eat. There's nothing there to eat, nothing there to feed them or, what, I don't know. I don't know, it's stupid, it's fucking retarded. I'm so sick of this origami shit.

ILANA: Why? Why are you so angry?

SURESH: This is the stupidest shit in the world. Doves. And paper cranes. And a whole conference and everything, all just for origami. What a waste of time.

ILANA: It's not a waste of time.

SURESH: Whatever. Like you even fold anyhow. I've never seen you fold a single thing. Supposed to be your apprentice or something, and what have you even taught me or shown me? Nothing. Don't talk to me about how awesome origami is if you can't even fold one piece of stupid paper.

> *They are silent for a moment. Suresh stares out the window. Long beat. Ilana watches him as he stares out the window.*

SURESH: My mom got hit by a car.
That's how she died.

ILANA: I know.

SURESH: Those kids fold doves as if it means anything. It doesn't mean anything.
And I'm at the epicenter today and I fold some stupid birds and everyone acts like I did something profound or meaningful, but it's not, it's not profound, it doesn't mean anything. It doesn't mean anything except that I know how to fold paper.
Fuck all this. I'm serious. Fuck all this.

Ilana picks up a square piece of folding paper from the bed, looks at it, pushes it toward Suresh.

ILANA: Look at this.

Look at this paper. It has no memory, it's just flat.

But fold it, even once, and suddenly it remembers something.

And then with each fold, another memory, another experience, and they build up to make something complicated.

The paper must forget that it was ever flat, ever a simple square.

It probably can't remember it's still in one piece.

Probably feels like too many things have happened to it. It's all twisted into something so far from what it used to be.

I guess it could unfold and become flat again. But it would never be what it was.

When it was untouched.

Folds leave scars.

SURESH: Show me your fist.

> *Ilana puts her fist out. Suresh puts his hand around it.*

SURESH: Tomorrow, we should check out the fish.

ILANA: We should.

> *He holds her fist.*

SURESH: Your heart's not beating.

> *Ilana starts squeezing her fist like a heartbeat, like Suresh did.*

> *Suresh takes her fist in both hands. He holds her fist and then kisses it.*

> *He looks at her and leans in and kisses her.*

SURESH: I'm sorry.

ILANA: No . . .

SURESH: I just . . . I don't know.

ILANA: It's okay.

> *Beat. They look at each other.*

SURESH: Can I kiss you again?

ILANA: I don't know.
No.

SURESH: Why not?

ILANA: You don't want to kiss me.

SURESH: Yeah I do.

> *He kisses her again.*

SURESH: This city is crazy.

> *He tries to kiss her again. But she backs away.*
> *She takes his face in her hands and she kisses his*
> *forehead.*

SURESH: I'm sorry . . . I . . .

ILANA: Shh. It's okay. It's okay.

> *Suresh falls into her. Ilana holds him, folding him into*
> *her, close to her. She holds him, stroking his face. She*
> *looks at him, and then out toward the city.*

Scene 3.

> *Ilana's studio.*

> *Andy has prepared a little meal. Basket of bread,*
> *some cheese, fruit, wine. A tablecloth on the table,*
> *flowers in a vase. He's putting the finishing touches*
> *on it when Suresh enters.*

ANDY: Oh.

SURESH: Oh. What up Fro Dog?

ANDY: Suresh? What are you doing here?

SURESH: I don't know. I just got back from Japan.

ANDY: Where's Ilana?

SURESH: I thought she'd be here by now.

ANDY: Didn't you come from the airport together?

SURESH: No.

ANDY: So . . . Did you come here for . . . I mean . . . Can I get you something?

SURESH: I came over to, you know . . . she uh . . . she packed some of my stuff in her luggage cause I was out of space, so I came over to get it. What about you?

ANDY: Nothing. Just, you know. Thought Ilana and I would eat a little dinner.

SURESH: Oh.

Awkward silence.

ANDY: Jeez! I'm sorry, buddy, do you want some bread?

SURESH: No thanks.

ANDY: It's got kalamata olives baked into it. Can you believe that?

SURESH: Naw, man. I'm cool.

ANDY: So? How was Japan?

SURESH: Japan was crazy.

ANDY: That's great!

SURESH: Yeah.

ANDY: And the conference?

SURESH: Crazy.

ANDY: Great!

SURESH: Yeah.

Awkward silence.

ANDY: I wonder where she is?

SURESH: Yeah.

Awkward silence.

ANDY: How was the flight?

SURESH: Awright.

ANDY: Was there a movie?

SURESH: I guess. I didn't really watch.

ANDY: I always thought, if I took a long trip, I'd watch all the movies.

SURESH: Yeah.

ANDY: Did Ilana have a good time?

SURESH: I guess.

ANDY: Are you okay?

SURESH: Huh? Yeah. Yeah, I'm cool.
Long flight, you know?

ANDY: Sure.
You must have had like two or three movies on that flight.

SURESH: Yeah.

ANDY: Did Ilana watch the movies?

SURESH: I dunno. We didn't sit together.

ANDY: You didn't? Why not?

SURESH: We did on the way over, but not on the way back. She,
um . . . She like upgraded her ticket? First class. And I was back in
coach. Economy style, you know?

ANDY: Wow. First class?

SURESH: They let the first class off the plane first. And so . . . I guess I figured she'd be here by now.

ANDY: Huh.

So she just . . . left you at the airport? That doesn't seem . . . I mean, that's strange.

SURESH: She's a strange lady.

ANDY: Did you piss her off again?

SURESH: Not that I know of.

We got up this morning to leave? And she was . . . I don't know. She sort of told me that, you know . . . that this thing was finished.

ANDY: What thing?

SURESH: You know, like my apprenticeship. My senior project. She told me I was done. That I should, you know, stop coming here and everything.

ANDY: But why?

SURESH: You tell me, man. I don't understand anything she does.

ANDY: *I* don't understand her. I mean . . . I don't understand her at all.

SURESH: Bitch.

ANDY: *(sternly)* Hey. Watch it.

SURESH: I'm just saying.

ANDY: You don't call Ilana that.

SURESH: I know.

ANDY: Don't use that word, Suresh. Just don't use it.

SURESH: I know.

ANDY: So . . . what about your senior project.

SURESH: It's over. She gave me an A. I'm done, man.
I'm done with high school.

ANDY: Well . . . Congratulations.

SURESH: Yeah. Yeah, thanks.
It's just that, you know . . .
I don't know.
I don't want to be done with high school.
I liked high school, you know?

ANDY: I know.

SURESH: I'll never forget this time in my life.

ANDY: I know.

Beat.

ANDY: You're going to be okay, you know Suresh?

SURESH: I don't know.

ANDY: What. What don't you know?

SURESH: *(quietly)* I'm having kind of a rough time.

ANDY: *(very concerned)*
Why? What? What's going on?

SURESH: I don't know, man.

ANDY: Come here, buddy. What's going on with you?

Suresh shrugs.

ANDY: Japan was good, right? I mean, it sounds like you had a great time . . .

SURESH: I liked Japan, you know, the origami thing? The conference? I learned a lot.
But Nagasaki, man, it's kind of a weird place. I felt like I was kind of a different person there. And I think Ilana did too. And for one week, I got to be someone else. And now I'm back to being me. Except I still remember being someone else, and I don't know. It's like I'm two things at once. But I shouldn't be. Nobody should be. You should be one thing at once.
(beat; Suresh looks around him) I love this place.
It's like a paper zoo.

They both look around at everything.

ANDY: I know.

Beat.

SURESH: I never would have met her if you hadn't, you know . . . You brought me here.

ANDY: I'm glad this was good for you.

SURESH: I don't know if it was good for me.
But I definitely feel different.

ANDY: Suresh, look at me.

Suresh does.

ANDY: You're amazing to me.
You're the most exceptional student I've ever had and I don't know if I taught you anything, but I've learned a lot from watching you. You're brave. You have smarts, sure. But it's your heart. It's big and strong and it's going to serve you well. So listen to it. It's a reliable narrator, you understand me?

SURESH: Yeah.

ANDY: You're done with high school now, but if you ever need anything . . . I mean *anything* . . . you come to me. You come to me, buddy.

Suresh covers his face for a moment, and paces around, racked with guilt.

SURESH: Aw shit, man.

ANDY: What's wrong?

SURESH: I feel really bad about things, Fro Dog. I'm sorry. I feel really bad.

ANDY: About what?

SURESH: I don't know.
Sometimes I just don't know how to act around people.

ANDY: I know what you mean.

Beat.

ANDY: I count my blessings.

SURESH: Yeah, I should do that, too.

ANDY: No, I literally count them.
(takes out his book) I've been doing it since I was twelve. When I think of one, I write it down in this book.
(opens it) Number 1: My health.
That's pretty basic.
Number 2: I can still go bowling, even with my elbow.
I just count them.

SURESH: You write them down? How many you got?

Andy hands him the book. Suresh flips through it.

ANDY: I number them. I have like over eight thousand blessings in here.
It helps. It's just a nice thing to do.
You should try it.

Suresh finds one and reads it.

SURESH: "Number 4,722: I bought a really excellent rake. It rakes really well. All the leaves just get raked, but they don't get stuck in the rake. And it wasn't that expensive."
(he looks up at Andy) Fro Dog . . . A rake?

ANDY: Hey, I'm just saying . . . keep your eyes peeled.

Suresh hands the book back to Andy.

SURESH: Mr. Froling . . .

ANDY: *Mr. Froling?*

SURESH: When the school year started . . . you know . . . I dropped out of Calc Club . . .

ANDY: Come on, it's okay.

SURESH: I'm sorry. I'm sorry. I always liked Calc Club.

ANDY: Calc Club always liked you.

SURESH: Yeah.
Also? Mr. Froling?

ANDY: Why do you keep calling me that?

> *Ilana enters.*
>
> *She's startled by everyone in her place.*

SURESH: Yo.

ILANA: What's going on here?!

ANDY: Well, I made dinner. And then Suresh stopped by, and . . .

ILANA: Suresh, what's going on?

SURESH: Nothing.

ILANA: You startled me.

ANDY: We were just chatting.

ILANA: *(to Suresh)* What are you doing here?

SURESH: Why'd you have to ditch me at the airport?

ILANA: I didn't ditch you. I just left.

SURESH: I wanted to talk to you.

ILANA: Well, we can't talk right now.

SURESH: Why are you being this way?

ILANA: Suresh . . . Please . . . let's just . . . Just let this go. Let it go.

SURESH: I don't want to let it go.

ILANA: You have to.

ANDY: Boy, you guys are like jet-lagged or something. Why doesn't everyone just relax? Let's have some food. Look, I've got a tapenade.

ILANA: Suresh, nothing happened. Nothing happened.

SURESH: *Something* happened. I don't know what, but things are different now.

ANDY: Can someone tell me what's going on?

> *A beat. Andy and Suresh look to Ilana to explain.*

ILANA: Can I take a moment to gather my thoughts? I mean, we just got home, can I just . . . can I sit here for a second?

> *Ilana sits on the couch. Suresh and Andy both look at her. A beat.*

SURESH: I know you're wigging out.

ILANA: I'm not wigging out.

SURESH: I'm just saying, last night . . . last night . . .
    I don't know what the word is.

ANDY: Um . . . what exactly happened last night?

SURESH: It wasn't even really "last night" what with the time change and everything. I think. I'm all messed up with my internal clock.

ILANA: You're reading into something that wasn't there. I'm sorry if you're confused, but nothing happened.

SURESH: Nothing happened? We kissed. We slept in the same bed. We woke up all tangled up with each other. That happened.

ANDY: *What?*

SURESH: Fro Dog, I'm sorry, man.

ANDY: What do you mean you kissed?

ILANA: Suresh! Andy, we didn't kiss.

SURESH: Yeah we did. We kissed twice. Three times, even.

ILANA: I mean, we did, briefly, but it wasn't a real kiss . . .

ANDY: You kissed him?

ILANA: It wasn't . . . it wasn't inappropriate. Or maybe it was, but Andy, you have to listen to me . . .

ANDY: I'm listening.

SURESH: Fro Dog . . .

> *Andy puts his hand up, to quiet Suresh.*

ILANA: It isn't what you think . . .

ANDY: I don't think anything right now. Except that you . . . *kissed* . . . my *student* . . . You *slept* . . . you *slept* with him?

ILANA: No! Not like that! We fell asleep in the same bed. Look, it was a strange moment. But it didn't mean anything.

ANDY: Ilana . . . We're talking about my student here. I brought you my *student*. I entrusted to you a kid who . . . this *kid* . . . this *kid* . . . Ilana!

ILANA: Nothing happened!

ANDY: This is like predatory!

ILANA: It wasn't predatory.

ANDY: Yes it is!

ILANA: Suresh, was it predatory?

SURESH: Naw.

ILANA: See?

ANDY: Shut up, Suresh! The adults are talking right now. *The adults, Ilana.*

ILANA: It was this weird moment between us. But nothing happened. I held him. I just held him.

ANDY: You *held* him? Do you know what would happen to me if I *held* a student?

ILANA: Andy, you're not getting this . . .

ANDY: I'd be fired! Because it crosses a line! To say nothing of *kissing* and *sleeping in the same bed* in a *hotel*! Lines *crossed*, Ilana! Lines *crossed*!

ILANA: Okay! But Andy, you weren't there! You don't understand the situation!

ANDY: I don't need to!

ILANA: Yes you do! Because I'm not . . . Suresh and I have a different relationship . . .

ANDY: No you don't! That was not part of the agreement! He comes to you to do a senior project . . . You take him to Nagasaki . . . I mean, the way you painted that . . . he's your *protégé* . . . he's your *apprentice* . . . he'd learn so *much*. I hardly thought this was the kind of education you had in mind.

SURESH: Yo, Fro Dog . . .

ANDY: Don't "Fro Dog" me!

SURESH: It was different. I mean, it was weird, but I kissed her, she didn't kiss me.

ILANA: You see? Nothing happened.

SURESH: No, something happened! I kissed you!

ILANA: And I kissed you back and it was wrong and I wanted . . . I wanted something *but I didn't take it!*

ANDY: He's *seventeen years old!*

SURESH: I'm eighteen.

ILANA: He's eighteen.

ANDY: He's a kid! For God's sake, Ilana, he's a kid!

ILANA: I did the right thing!

> *Andy paces, not knowing what to do with himself.*

ANDY: I don't understand how you can . . .

SURESH: Fro Dog, man . . . I'm sorry . . .
I don't know what happened.

It was a crazy night. I feel like I was an insect and I molted.
I mean, it's why I came here today, Ilana. I just need to talk to you.
I molted and now I don't recognize myself.

ILANA: Yeah, well, welcome to the rest of your life.

ANDY: No. No, you don't say that to him. Suresh, you go ahead and
you figure this out, like you figure everything out. You're always going
to recognize yourself. That's your gift, buddy. Don't let her tell you
different.
She doesn't know.

ILANA: It was a *kiss*! It was just a kiss! It doesn't mean anything!

ANDY: It doesn't mean anything?
(he takes out his book) I've been counting my blessings my whole
life. Putting them in this book.
But the best blessing I ever wrote in here, the blessing that made
me feel the most *blessed* was number 7,906.
(he reads it) Ilana Andrews kissed me.
Ilana Andrews kissed me.
Ilana Andrews kissed me.
(he looks up) I had to write it three times.

ILANA: Andy . . .

ANDY: What a *joke*.

ILANA: Can you please calm down?

ANDY: I'm trying! I'm trying to figure out why I shouldn't feel totally
betrayed right now, but I can't. I'm sorry, I can't.

ILANA: But you do it all the time! Your book, you're always finding the
silver lining, finding blessings in the worst things . . .

ANDY: It's not easy, okay?! It doesn't just *happen*. It takes time. It takes
time for me to do that.

He flips through the pages.

ANDY: I don't just sit around thinking everything is perfect all the time.
(he rips a page out) This stuff is just . . . it's just . . . it's not all true,
it's things I hope for!

(he rips another page out) But what is it anyway? Nothing. It means nothing.

> *Andy starts ripping more pages out of his book, tearing his book up.*

ILANA: What are you doing!

ANDY: Just take it. Take it, take it, take it, take it, take it.

> *A pile of pages on the floor.*

ILANA: Andy . . . don't do this! Please, don't, I made a mistake, okay? Just don't do this!

ANDY: I never wanted you to read that. It was every last thing about me and you read it and then you just walk away and you humiliate me. So keep it. Keep it all, but I have to leave.

> *Andy exits.*
>
> *Ilana, holding some loose papers, drops them, runs to the door after Andy, but he's gone.*
>
> *Ilana doesn't move. She stands at the doorway for a long moment.*
>
> *Suresh starts to gather up the papers.*

ILANA: Stop. Don't do that.

SURESH: I'm just gonna pick them up.

ILANA: *Stop it! Suresh!* Don't pick them up! I swear to God, don't pick them up!

> *Suresh continues to pick up the papers, quickly.*
>
> *Ilana goes to him and grabs his face like a child.*

ILANA: What did I say to you!? Put those down! Put them down! Drop the papers, Suresh. Drop them *now.* Let them go. Let go of the paper.

Let go.
Let go now.

> *Suresh puts his hand over hers and holds it to his face for a moment and drops the papers.*

ILANA: It's not your mess. You don't need to clean it up.

SURESH: I want to.

ILANA: It's not yours to clean.

SURESH: Fro Dog wrote his blessings in that book! That stuff is important! You should at least pick it up. That would be the right thing to do, you know?

ILANA: You need to go. You need to go home now. I can't help you. I'm sorry I never could. Everything I touch I hurt.

SURESH: Not me.
(*beat*) Not me, Ilana.
You didn't hurt me.

> *Ilana doesn't answer. She looks through the pages.*

SURESH: I gotta start doing that. Counting my blessings and everything. Fro Dog, he's usually right about things, you know?
My health. Got that. Got to remember that.
Meeting you.
Coming here.
Hanging with you in the afternoons and everything.
Blessings.
You know.
Meeting you.
Going to Japan with you.
Nagasaki.
Folding you stuff.
Little rabbits, dogs, T. rexes, little birds I folded for you.
Being able to come here. Meeting you. Knowing you.
You hooked me up this semester.
That's a blessing, you know?

I gotta remember it. I always will.

> *Suresh gets his bags and starts to leave, but looks at her.*
>
> *They look at each other. She raises a fist to him. He bumps it with his fist. He exits.*
>
> *After a beat, Ilana goes to the pages on the floor and gathers them up very carefully.*
>
> *She takes them to her desk and puts them on the desk, looking through them.*
>
> *She takes a piece of folding paper and returns to the couch. She stares at the paper and then slowly makes a single fold.*

BENGAL TIGER
AT THE
BAGHDAD ZOO

PRODUCTION HISTORY

Bengal Tiger at the Baghdad Zoo had its world premiere on May 10, 2009, at the Kirk Douglas Theatre in Culver City, California, in a production by Center Theatre Group. Moisés Kaufman, Director; Derek McLane, Sets; David Zinn, Costumes; David Lander, Lighting; Cricket S. Myers, Sound; Kathryn Bostic, Music; Bobby C. King, Fight Director; Vanessa J. Noon, Production Stage Manager.

TIGER: Kevin Tighe
TOM: Glenn Davis
KEV: Brad Fleischer
MUSA: Arian Moayed
UDAY/MAN: Hrach Titizian
HADIA/IRAQI TEENAGER: Sheila Vand
IRAQI WOMAN/LEPER (WOMAN 2): Necar Zadegan

CHARACTERS

TIGER: big *(Tiger wears clothes. Nothing feline about him.)*
TOM: American, early twenties, older and wiser than Kev, unsmiling, tough
KEV: American, early twenties
MUSA: Iraqi, thirties
WOMAN 1: Iraqi
WOMAN 2: Iraqi
UDAY: Iraqi, thirties
HADIA (GIRL): Iraqi teenager

TIME

2003

SETTING

Baghdad

NOTE

Tiger can be any age, although, ideally, he is older, scrappy, past his prime, yet still tough. He can be any race except Middle Eastern. His language is loose, casual; his profanity is second nature.

There should be no subtitles for the Arabic.

ACT 1
Scene 1.

The Baghdad Zoo, night.

Two American soldiers standing guard next to a cage with a Bengal tiger.

The tiger stands like a person and faces and speaks to the audience.

TIGER: The lions escaped two days ago. Predictably, they got killed in about two hours. Everyone always gives lions so much credit. But I am bigger than them. I am bigger than those motherfuckers.

TOM: This guy is hungry.

KEV: Sergeant said they fed him.

TIGER: They liked to show off the lions here because they had eight.

TOM: No, he's hungry.

TIGER: Eight fucking lions.

KEV: This place creeps me out. I wanna see some action, not hang around no ghetto-ass zoo with my thumb up my ass.

TIGER: Which is why they had them in that big outdoor lions' den. Which is why they all got away.

TOM: Zoo duty's seen action three nights last week.

KEV: Who's gonna attack a zoo.

TOM: *We're* here. They'll attack *us*. And they've been stealing shit. Like peacocks.

TIGER: All eight of them took off as soon as the wall got blown up.

KEV: I don't know why they wanna kill *us*. We're trying to protect their zoo, you know?

TIGER: Typical lionlike behavior.

TOM: *We* blew the zoo up. Use your head. And these animals are valuable.

TIGER: Three square meals a day, and they take off.

KEV: This guy ain't valuable.
  So let me see it.

TOM: Again?

KEV: C'mon, Tommy. Let me see it.

TOM: I showed you it already.

KEV: I wanna fire it!

TOM: You're not gonna fire anything.

TIGER: And what happens?

KEV: Come on, man.

TOM: It's not even loaded.

KEV: You told me you always keep it loaded.

TIGER: *Ka-boom.*

TOM: Well, you're not gonna fire it anyway.

TIGER: I mean, it's the middle of a war. Use your head.

TOM: How many times you gonna want to see it?

KEV: It's badass.

TIGER: Leo, the head lion—I mean, they were all named fucking Leo—Leo calls out to me just before he takes off, "Hey, Tiger, you gotta come with!"

KEV: I wrote my brother about it. He said there ain't no such thing as no gold gun. He said guns can't be made outta gold.

The boys hear a sound.

KEV: What the fuck was that?

TIGER: I said, Leo, you dumb stupid bastard, they're killing anything that *moves*. And Leo—this is right over his head—he yells back, *Suit yourself!* Then he runs off.

TOM: *(picks up his machine gun)*
Halt! Who goes there!

KEV: *(yelling, picking up his gun)*

Who's there? We're U.S. Marines!

TOM: Shut up, Kev.
(shouts) Advance and be recognized!
(to Kev) Cover me.

> Tom exits.

TIGER: *I gotta come with.* I'm still freaking locked up in here, Leo! What're you gonna do, steal the keys and *let me out*? These lions were dumb as rocks. They think because they can suddenly escape, everyone else can too.

> Tom enters.

TOM: It was that fucking ostrich.

KEV: You shoulda shot it.

TOM: I'm not gonna kill an ostrich.

KEV: Fuck that, man. I don't give a fuck. I'll be like . . .
(he pretends to shoot his machine gun) What's up ostrich, motherfucker? I'll *kill* you, bitch!

TOM: At ease with that shit.
This is why everyone thinks you're a fucking idiot, you know that?

KEV: That's what *I'd* do, anyway.

TOM: Sergeant said no more killing animals unless they're a danger.

KEV: Sergeant is a pussy.
Can I see it?

TOM: It's in my bag, Kev! Just get it!

Kev darts to Tom's canvas satchel and pulls out a
gold-plated semiautomatic pistol.

KEV: Holy shit, man.

TIGER: I won't lie. When I get hungry, I get stupid. I screwed up twelve years back. I just followed the scent, took a bite, and then, *fhwipp!*

KEV: A gold fuckin gun.

TIGER: This tranquilizer dart comes out of nowhere, and I wake up in Baghdad.

KEV: Sweet ass.

TIGER: So that was depressing.

TOM: You happy now?

KEV: Hell yeah!

TIGER: Imagine, it's your everyday routine . . . maybe you want to grab a bite, and then *whack!*

KEV: Yeah, this is the shit right here.

TIGER: Curtains.

KEV: You swear to God this was really Saddam's kid's gun?

TIGER: And you open your eyes and you're in this concrete block.

TOM: Uday.

KEV: Who?

TOM: Uday Hussein.

KEV: Who's that?

TIGER: Tiger of the Tigris.

TOM: Saddam's kid.

KEV: Damn.

TIGER: When you're this far from home, you know you're never getting back.

KEV: This really his gun?

TOM: Yes it was his gun. Who else has a gold-plated gun?

KEV: Damn.

TOM: *(looking at the tiger)*
Look at this poor bastard. He's hungry.
(to Tiger) You hungry, buddy?

> *Tom hits the cage.*

TOM: Hey buddy!

TIGER: Yeah, fuck you too.

TOM: Goddamn! You hear that growl, baby? He's starving.

KEV: How you know for sure? How you know that it was Saddam's kid's gun?

TOM: We raided the mansion. I was there, man. Two-day standoff.

KEV: Fuuuck . . .

TIGER: Anyhow, what if my cage *had* gotten hit? What if, *Ka-boom*, there's a big gaping hole in my cage? What do I do then?
I'm not gonna go traipsing around the city, like the lions did. No, fuck that.

KEV: What mansion?

TOM: The Hussein brothers' *mansion*, jackass. Uday and Qusay. They were stacked with gold and shit. Everything in the house was made of gold, practically.

TIGER: But I think I'd step out for a bit. Hang around the zoo. Hunt something. Kill all the people, kill everyone. Eat them.

KEV: What else was gold?

TOM: All their guns. Sergeant got the gold UZI.

TIGER: Then I'd sleep a little. And then get up, kill some of the animals. Eat them. Sleep some more. But I guess at that point, I'd probably step out. Into the world. Not like the lions did, but still, have to admit, I'm curious.

TOM: The toilet was made of gold.

KEV: No shit. The shitter?

TIGER: The world is probably a fascinating place.

TOM: The *toilet* was gold. Sergeant dismantled the whole thing.
I won the seat off him in poker.

KEV: You won a toilet seat?

TOM: *Gold* toilet seat. I won the *gold* toilet seat.

KEV: Where is it.

TOM: Somewhere real safe. I buried it.

KEV: Where?

TOM: Yeah, I'm gonna tell you, Kev. I'm gonna tell *you*.
Somewhere safe.
Between this gun and that toilet seat, I am set. Back home, I'll be
sitting pretty.

KEV: Sitting pretty on a gold toilet seat!

TOM: No, dude. I'm not going to *use* it. I'm gonna hit eBay with that
shit, you know?

KEV: Man.
I haven't seen nothing since I been here.

TIGER: Zoo is hell. Ask any animal. Rather be shot up and eaten than
be stuck in a fucking zoo ten thousand miles from where you were
supposed to be. Like that polar bear they brought in six years ago who
committed suicide. Some world.

KEV: You got to kill Saddam's kids, man. That's awesome.

TOM: Yeah, it was cool.

TIGER: And the fucking lions! They get it *all*, right? Every captive
animal's dream: that a bolt of lightning comes down and *zap!* Frees
you in an instant. There it was: freedom! And they blew it. They
walked right into the mouth of the beast. Dumb sons of bitches. It's
too iffy strutting out into the world like that. I can see them: the eight
Leos running through the streets of Baghdad, laughing their heads off.

And then—*Ka-boom*—mowed down by artillery. Casualties. A pride of fucking lions.

KEV: I ain't seen shit. Nothing. Not one Iraqi did I get to kill! And I ain't got my dick wet neither! You know back in Vietnam, there was so many Vietnamese bitches all over the place, and everyone got a piece.

TOM: You weren't even born yet.

KEV: I'm just saying. Not much pussy in a Muslim country.

TOM: Sergeant got some. Sergeant gets that shit all the time.

KEV: You ever get any Iraqi pussy?

TOM: No, man. Fuck that. I got values.
Hand me that Slim Jim.

> *Kev hands Tom a Slim Jim. Tom unwraps it and sticks it through the cage, trying to poke Tiger.*

TOM: Dumb bastard is so hungry, he don't even know he's hungry.

KEV: Leave him alone. He's barely got any fur left anyhow.

TOM: Eat! Eat it up, man!

TIGER: Don't wanna eat.

TOM: Come on, tough guy. Give me another growl.

TIGER: Leave me alone.

TOM: Atta boy. Get angry. Eat something.

TIGER: *(to audience)* This is what I'm talking about. Pure stupidity. I'm a fucking tiger.

> *Tom hits Tiger with the Slim Jim.*

TOM: *Eat!*

> *Tiger bites Tom's hand off.*

TOM: My hand!

TIGER: *(with mouth full)* Yeah, your hand!

TOM: My fucking hand!

TIGER: Yum yum yum . . .

> *Kev shoots the tiger repeatedly with the gold gun.*

TOM: Oh God, my hand!

KEV: Tommy! Tommy, you okay?
(beat) I shot him, Tommy! I shot him!

> *Tom collapses and passes out.*
>
> *The tiger, now a ghost, stands outside the cage and can watch as Kev walks over to the cage, pointing the gun at the tiger's dead body.*

KEV: I fucking shot him! I shot him! Oh my God I shot him!

TIGER: Great. This is just wonderful. I get so stupid when I get hungry! Starts out with a tranquilizer dart. Ends with a bullet.

KEV: He's dead, Tommy! I killed him!

> *Beat.*

TIGER: To die in captivity at the Baghdad Zoo. What a freaking life.

KEV: Who's king of the jungle *now?*

TIGER: The lions, you jackass.

KEV: Man down! Man attacked by fucking tiger animal!
I'm gonna go get help, Tommy! Stay here! *(gets on radio)*

> *Kev exits. Tiger stares at his own dead body.*
>
> *Beat.*

TIGER: But I guess I was always going to die here. I guess that was my fate, from the start.
But I would have thought maybe I'd have one good day. A day like the Leos had. A brief foray out into the great wide open.

And I'm bigger than them. I am bigger than those motherfuckers.
So that's what I look like. You go your whole life never knowing
how you look. And then there you are. You get hungry, you get stupid,
you get shot and die. And you get this quick glimpse at how you look,
to those around you, to the world. It's never what you thought. And
then it's over.

Curtains.

Ka-boom.

Scene 2.

> *Musa sits on the floor in an office, writing. There is
> a laptop to his side and a dictionary.*

> *He writes and then reads what he writes.*

MUSA: "Knock, knock."
"Who's there?"
"Operation Iraqi Freedom."
"Operation Iraqi Freedom who?"
"Operation Iraqi Freedom . . . *bitch.*"

> *Musa stares at the words, shakes his head,
> frustrated, confused.*

> *He flips through the dictionary.*

MUSA: "Bitch . . . bitch . . . "

> *He finds the word. Reads it. Frowns and shakes his
> head and puts the book aside.*

> *Kev enters carrying a huge amount of combat gear.*

> *He puts it down and catches his breath. Musa stares
> at him. Kev stares back.*

MUSA: What is "bitch"?

KEV: What?

MUSA: "Bitch." What is "bitch"?

KEV: Are you calling me a bitch?

MUSA: No. I am asking you what "bitch" means.

KEV: So why you calling me a bitch, bitch?

MUSA: I want to know what it means. "Bitch." The word. I look it up in the dictionary.

Kev starts donning his gear.

KEV: You're the terp.

MUSA: Yes. My name is Musa.

KEV: You going on the night raids?

MUSA: Yes.

KEV: You speak Iraqi?

MUSA: Arabic.

KEV: *Arabic?*

MUSA: Iraqi Arabic.

KEV: So why do you get a computer?

MUSA: This computer?

KEV: No, Habib, the other computer. The other computer in here.

Beat. Musa looks at Kev, confused.

KEV: Yes, that computer!

MUSA: This is my own computer. I bought it.

Beat.

KEV: It have a DVD player?

MUSA: DVD? Yes.

KEV: You got any movies?

MUSA: Movies? Yes. I have a number of movies.

KEV: What movies you got?

MUSA: I have a number of movies. I have *Fast and Furious.*

KEV: You got *Fast and Furious?*

MUSA: Yes.

KEV: I love that movie.

MUSA: It's a good film.

KEV: Great fucking movie.

MUSA: Yes.
  (beat) What is this word "bitch"?

KEV: Why you keep asking me about "bitch"?

MUSA: I know the word. It is derogatory, meaning the female of the dog. But I do not always understand its context. I have looked it up in the dictionary.

KEV: So what's it say in the *dictionary?* Jesus!

MUSA: There are a number of definitions
  (reads) "The female of the dog."
  "A spiteful or domineering woman."
  "To complain of or about."

KEV: But it also means, you know, like you're a faggot ass or something.

MUSA: Again, this I don't quite understand.

KEV: You know, like if you're a little pussy or something, or you're being like, you know, a pussy. Then you're being a bitch, you know?

MUSA: No.

KEV: Why do want to know anyway?

MUSA: I speak English, but I don't understand casual American phrases. So when I go with the soldiers, I listen for these phrases and I write them down so that I can better understand the way you speak. It's also why I enjoy watching films.

KEV: You learning English from *The Fast and the Furious*?

MUSA: I watch *The Fast and the Furious* because of the cars. I like the cars.

KEV: Yeah, they're sweet ass.

MUSA: But I overheard this the other day. It is a joke.
Knock, knock.

KEV: Who's there?

MUSA: Operation Iraqi Freedom.

KEV: Operation Iraqi Freedom who?

MUSA: Operation Iraqi Freedom, *bitch*.

KEV: Dah. That's good.

MUSA: What does "bitch" mean in this instance?

KEV: Well, we got these things called knock-knock jokes, right? And they're . . .

MUSA: No I understand the convention of knock-knock jokes.

KEV: So what's your question? Jesus. I mean, if you're such a smart guy.

MUSA: Never mind.

Kev finishes putting on his combat gear.

KEV: Fuck yeah.
Fuck yeah.

MUSA: Why have you dressed in here?

KEV: None of your business, Habib.

MUSA: I mean, this is just office space. Just translators work in here. Why would you dress in here?

KEV: None of your fucking business, I said.

MUSA: Are you new?

KEV: I'm not new.

MUSA: No?

KEV: I've seen action, boy.

MUSA: Me too.

KEV: Yeah, but I have a gun. You, what *you* do, you *talk.*

MUSA: I help you do your job.

KEV: You don't help me with shit, Habib.

MUSA: I see.

KEV: That's why I get this badass equipment, see? And that's why you get a fucking laptop. You can boot up and watch *Fast and Furious*, but I live it, bitch. I *live Fast and Furious.*

MUSA: Why am I a bitch?

KEV: Just shut up.

MUSA: What kind of action have you seen?

KEV: What kind?

MUSA: Yes.

KEV: I killed a tiger.

MUSA: You killed . . . ?

KEV: A tiger. At the zoo.

MUSA: I see. Why?

KEV: He bit off my friend's hand! This tiger, he attacked him, this guy Tommy, he's like my best friend over here. And so I shot the bastard in the gut. *Bucka bucka!* The tiger, I mean. And he died.
　　I saved Tommy's life, you know? But everyone's like . . . Everyone's all like . . . I screwed up or something. Like I did something wrong.
　　I wanted to get the tiger and skin him. I wanted to make a carpet out of him, but they wouldn't let me. Can you believe that?

MUSA: Yes, you got gypped.

KEV: That's right! I got fucking gypped!

MUSA: That is one of the casual phrases I have learned.

> *Kev laughs and smiles at Musa.*

KEV: Hey. You want to see something?

MUSA: Yes.

KEV: You can't tell anyone you saw this, okay?

MUSA: Okay.

KEV: I'm serious, Habib.

MUSA: Yes.

> *Kev looks around covertly. Goes into his bag, pulls out the gold gun. He shows it to Musa.*

KEV: You see this shit?
  This was Saddam's kid's gun.

MUSA: What?

KEV: Saddam's kid. I don't know. Last name Hussein.

> *Musa stares at the gun. He reaches out for it.*

KEV: Uh-uh. No touchy, Habib.

MUSA: May I?

KEV: No touchy.

MUSA: I would just like to . . . please. May I hold it?

> *Kev considers. He likes that Musa wants it.*

KEV: Okay, but don't get any ideas, Habib. I will waste you.

> *Musa takes the gun and stares at it.*

KEV: I was at the standoff at the palace, baby. Two-day standoff. We killed those sons of bitches. Both of them. Man, that palace they had? Gold out the ass, man. Gold everywhere. All their weapons were gold! Even their toilet was gold, boy! Goddamn!

> *Musa still stares at the gun, now grasping it in a strange manner. He begins to shake with rage.*

KEV: Dude. Habib?

MUSA: You killed them?

KEV: Who?

MUSA: Uday Hussein. Qusay Hussein. You were among the soldiers who killed them?

KEV: Yeah, dude.
    What?

> *Musa shakes, begins to breathe harshly.*

KEV: What is *wrong* with you, man?
    Dude! Relax!

> *Musa falls into a crouch, still clutching the gun.*
>
> *Kev tries to grab the gun from him.*

KEV: Habib, you're going psycho jihadi on me now, dude. Give me the gun! What the fuck?

> *Kev struggles to take the gun from Musa and finally does.*

KEV: Jesus! What the fuck is your problem?

> *Musa sits on the ground motionless, staring at nothing.*

KEV: Seriously, Habib. Are you going crazy on me here? Do I need to shoot you?

MUSA: You do not need to shoot me.

KEV: Good, man. Cause I don't want to shoot you.
   What's your problem, though?

MUSA: I don't have a problem.

KEV: No? Then what was all that shit about? All that shaking around and shit?
   (near tears) Jesus! Everything I see every day is just one crazy fucking thing after another. You're a freak, Habib. Freaky deaky, no shit.

> *Kev begins to freak out, shaking, nervous.*

MUSA: Please leave me alone.
   Please leave me.
   This room is for translators.
   Why are you here?

KEV: I got to get dressed!

MUSA: *(deliberate)*
Go. Dress. Somewhere. Else.

> *Beat.*

KEV: I just need to be alone when I put this stuff on or I don't do it right.
   It doesn't mean I'm a fucking idiot. I just have to concentrate.
   (beat) You know what I'm saying? This is like fifty pounds of gear, man. Kevlar and shit. It's like complicated, you know?

MUSA: Complicated.

KEV: Yeah. Complicated.
   It's war, you know? Everything is all fucked up. But see? Now I'm all set. Gonna go out tonight and figure some shit out, right?

MUSA: I suppose so.

> *Kev holds out his hand for a high five. Musa just looks at it.*

KEV: I catch you later, Habib.
Come on, man. High five.

Musa just stares at Kev's hand.

KEV: Come on, man! High five!

Musa lightly high-fives him.

KEV: That's what I'm talking about, bitch.
That's what I'm talking about.

Kev leaves, Musa watches him go.

Scene 3.

In the dark, chaotic sounds of soldiers pounding on the doors of a home. Yelling, screaming, furniture being overturned.

As the sounds continue, lights up on an Iraqi man standing with a sack tied around his head and his hands tied behind his back.

Kev enters with Musa.

A woman runs onstage and goes to the man. Her sudden entrance goes entirely against procedure and freaks Kev and Musa out.

WOMAN: *(Arabic) Don't take him! Get out of our house! Leave us alone!*

La-Takhthoo! Etle'oo min baitne! Joozoo min edne!

لا تــاخذوا! اطلـعو مـن بــيـتـنة! جوزو مـن عدنـة!

KEV: Whoa! Get her back!

MUSA: *(Arabic, to Woman) Go back!*

Irja-ee

ارجعي!

KEV: *(to Man)* I need you down on the ground! Hands behind your—
Sir? *Sir?* I need you *down* on the *ground! Down* on the *ground!*

MUSA: *(Arabic, to Man) You need go down to—*

Inteh Tehtaj tinzil lil . . .

انتة تحتاج تنزل لل ....

KEV: Wait, what are you telling him?

MUSA: What?

WOMAN: *(Arabic) There's nothing here for you! Go away!*

Makoo shee elkoom ehna! Roohoo!

ماكو شي الكم اهنا! روحو!

KEV: What are you telling him?

WOMAN: *(Arabic) We have done nothing wrong. Go away!*

Me sawaine shee ghalatt. Roohoo!

ما سوينة شي غلط. روحو!

MUSA: I'm telling him what you said!

KEV: What the fuck?

MUSA: I'm *translating!*

KEV: *(to Man)* You speak English? Hey, sir, you speak fucking *English!?*

MAN: *What does he want? What's he saying?*

Hathe shee-yreed? Hathe shday-gool?

هاذة شيريد؟ هاذة شد يكول؟

WOMAN: *(Arabic) I don't know, they're wrecking the house. They want to take you away!*

Ma a'roof, daykhereboon ilbait. Yreedoon yakhthook wiyahoom!

ما اعرف، ديخربون البيت. يريدون ياخذوك ويا هم!

Kev pushes Man.

KEV: You speak fucking English I said!

MUSA: He doesn't speak English!

KEV: Fuck that, man. Tell him to kneel down. I'm gonna count from five! Five . . . four . . . three . . . two . . .

MUSA: *(over Kev, Arabic) He wants you both to kneel down.*

Yireed-kum thnain-nat-koom terka'oon.

يـريـدكم ثـنيـنـاتـكم تـركـعـون.

The man and woman kneel down. Kev bumps into a large wooden chest and nearly falls over.

KEV: Hey! What's in this chest here? Hey you speaka Englisha?

MUSA: They don't speak English! Stop yelling! You don't need to yell.

KEV: That's what you gotta do, man, or these towelheads will fuck you, man.

MUSA: Just tell me what you want to tell them and I will translate. Okay?

KEV: Don't fucking tell me my business, Habib.

WOMAN: *(Arabic) Oh my God, we've done nothing, but say what do you want? You want to take us all away? Get out! Get out of my home!*

Allahoo akbar, ehne me sawaine shee, bess kooloo shitreedoon? Treedoon takhthoone kulne? Etla'oo! Etla'oo min baitee!

الله اكبر، احنة مـا سويـنـة شـي، بـس كـولـو شتريـدون؟ تـريـدون تـاخذونـة كـلـنة؟ اطلـعـو بـرة! اطلـعـو مـن بـيـتي!

MAN: *(Arabic) Stop making trouble! We must do what they say!*

Kafee tse-ween masha-kil! lazim nse-wee lee-reedoo!

كـافي تـسويـن مـشـاكـل! لازم نـسوي لـيـريـدو!

KEV: *(yelling)* Shut up! What's in this box?

MUSA: *(Arabic) He wants to know what is in this box.*

Yireed yu'roof shinoo bil sundoog.

يـديـد يـعرف شنو بـلـصنـدوك .

WOMAN: *(Arabic) The box!? He wants the box? He can take it, take it!*
Just leave, get them all out! We haven't done anything wrong!

Il sendoog, yreed il sendoog? Yigder yakhooth il sendoog, ukhthe! bess
roohoo, telle'hum koolhum berre! ehne me sawaine shee ghalatt!

الـصنـدوك؟ يـزيـد الـصنـدوك؟ يـكدر يـاخذ الـصنـدوك،
اخذة ! بـس روحو، طلـعهم كـلـهم بـرة !احنه مـسويـنـه
شي غلط !

MUSA: She says there are . . .

(to Woman, Arabic) What did you say?

Shgil-tee?

شكـلـتي؟

KEV: Wait what?

WOMAN: *(Arabic) There's nothing in there! Blankets and nothing else!*

Makoo shee hnak! bess Buttaniat, makoo ghair shee!

مـاكو شي هنـاك ! بـس بطانـيـات مـاكو غير شي !

MUSA: Nothing! There's nothing—

KEV: That's bullshit. She said a lot more than "nothing." I don't speak
Iraqi, but she said a lot more than "nothing."

WOMAN: *(Arabic) He wants a box? Tell him to take the box! Take it and*
leave!

Yireed il sendoog? Gul-le khelee yakhooth il sendoog! Yakhthe we-
yrooh!

يـريـد الـصنـدوك؟ كـلة خلـي يـاخذ الـصنـدوك ! يـاخذة
و يـدوح !

MAN: *(Arabic) Be quiet! Don't make it worse!*

Sook-tee! let saw-weeheh engess!

سكتي ! لـتـسويـهة انكـس !

MUSA: *(to Man and Woman, Arabic) Please be quiet! Please!*

Raja'en sook-too! Reja'en!

رجاء سكتو! رجاء!

KEV: *(re: Man and Woman talking)* See that's what I'm talking about.

> *Kev goes to Man and Woman and stands above
> them in a threatening manner.*

KEV: We are here to help you!

MUSA: You don't need to do this!

KEV: What's in the *box?!*

MUSA: *(to Woman, Arabic) What is in the box?*

Shinoo bil sundoog?

شنو بلصندوك؟

WOMAN: *(Arabic)*

Buttaniat! Buttaniat!

بطانيات! بطانيات!

MUSA: *(to Kev; accidentally in Arabic)*

Buttaniat!

بطانيات!

KEV: What? What the fuck did you say!?

MUSA: *(to Kev; in Arabic; frustrated)*

Buttaniat! Buttaniat!

بطانيات! بطانيات!

KEV: In *English!!* Speak English, will you?!

MUSA: What?

WOMAN: *(Arabic) Don't yell! Tell him to stop yelling! Leave us alone!*

Let suy-eh! gul-le kheli y-buttel y-suy-eh! Joozoo min edne!

لتصيح! كوله خلي يبطل يصيح! جوزو من عدنة!

KEV: What the fuck!

MAN: *(Arabic) Stop yelling!*

Kafee tsuy-heen!

كـا فـي تـصيـحـين!

MUSA: Blankets! Sorry! Blankets!

MAN: *(Arabic) There's nothing more for them to take! Just be quiet!*

Makoo ba'ad shee moomkin yakh-thoo! bess sook-tee!

مـاكـو بـعـد شـي ممكن يـاخـذو! بـس سكتي!

KEV: What blankets?!

MUSA: In the box!

KEV: What?

WOMAN: *(Arabic) Take it, steal it, steal everything we have. Criminals, all of you, every one of you.*

Ukhthoo, boogoo, boogu kulshee edne. Mujremeen, kulkum, kul wahid min edkum.

اخـذو، بـوكـو، بـوكـو كـلـشـي عـدنـة . مجرمـين، كـلـكـم، كـل
واحـد مـن عدكم .

MUSA: *Blankets! In the box!*

KEV: We'll see about that! We'll fucking see about that!

> *Kev walks to the chest and opens it and begins taking out folded blankets. He flaps them open and tosses them randomly.*

WOMAN: *(Arabic) What does he want? There's nothing there! They're blankets.*

Hathe Shee-yreed? Makoo shee hnak! Hethole buttaniat

هـاذة شيريـد؟ مـاكـو شـي هنـاك! هذولـه بـطـانـيـات

KEV: You see this!? You see?

MUSA: What!? What's wrong?! What's happened?

WOMAN: *(Arabic) They're just blankets!*

Hetholeh bess buttaniat!

هذولة بس بطانيات!

> As Kev goes through the blankets, he seems to be
> more and more desperate, looking for something in
> the box.

MUSA: You're supposed to stand guard!

KEV: I'm *supposed to do my job!*
Shut up!

WOMAN: *(Arabic) What is he doing? There's nothing there for him! He's
crazy! The man has lost his mind!*

Hathe shday-sa-wee? Makoo shee il-eh hnak! Hathe mejnoon! Hel-rijal
foo-ked akle!

هاذة شديسوي؟ ماكو شي اله هناك! هاذه مجنون! هل
رجال فقد عقله!

> Kev stares at one of the blankets, draped over
> a chair now. He paces around it, as if it might
> suddenly attack him. Something spooks him.
>
> He grabs the blanket and bunches it up and then
> throws it just as Tiger enters the scene. The blanket
> hits Tiger and clings to him. Kev sees this, but
> nobody else does.

KEV: Oh God, no way.

> Tiger seems to be almost sleepwalking, not aware
> of his surroundings. He shrugs the blanket off and
> wanders around, not sensing Kev or anyone else.
>
> Kev drops his gun. The woman screams.

MUSA: What's happened?! What are you doing?

> *Outside of the scene, a topiary hedge of animals is dimly lit and Tiger walks to it, examining it.*

MAN: *(Arabic) For God's sake what is going on? Come here! Come to me!*

Il khater alle hi shdayseer? Te'alee hna, te'alee yemmee!

الخاطر الله هاي شديصير؟ تعالي هنا! تعالي يمي!

MUSA: *(to Man and Woman, Arabic) Quiet! Will you shut up!*

Suntteh! moomkin tsooktoon!

صنطة! ممكن تسكتون!

WOMAN: *(Arabic) He's going to kill us! He's crazy!*

Hathe rah yuktulne! Hathe mejnoon!

هاذة رح يقتلنة! هاذة مجنون!

MAN: *(Arabic) What's happening? What's going on?*

Hi shday-seer? Hi shday-saw-woon?

هاي شديصير؟ هاي شديسوون؟

KEV: *Shut up!*

WOMAN: *(Arabic) Get him out of here! Oh, God ...*

Telle'a minna! Akh ya alla ...

طلعه منا! آخ يا الله....

KEV: *Nobody move! Nobody say a fucking word!*

MUSA: *(to Man and Woman, Arabic) Quiet!*

Suntteh!

صنطة !

> *Kev circles the chair with the blanket, takes out the gold gun from his uniform, pointing the gold gun at it.*

KEV: Motherfucker . . . motherfucker . . .

MUSA: *(yelling) What are you doing?!*

KEV: *Shut up!*

> *Kev picks up a blanket.*

KEV: You see this!?

> *He throws it.*

KEV: You see?
What the fuck is that!?

MUSA: That's a blanket.

KEV: What else, huh? What fucking else?!

MUSA: There's nothing there!

> *Kev points the gun at Musa. Woman screams.*

KEV: It's not a fucking blanket! It's him! It's *him!*

MUSA: I'm sorry!

> *Kev points the gun back at Tiger.*

MAN: *(Arabic) Come over here, come over here, what are they doing?*

Te'alee hna, te'alee hna, hethole shday-saw-woon?

تـعـالي هـنـا، تـعـالي هـنـا، هذولـة شديـسـوون؟

WOMAN: *(Arabic) I don't know! The soldier is sick in the head, he has his gun . . .*

Ma a'roof, hathe iljundee t-kheb-bell, oo ende museddess

مـا اعرف! هـاذة الجـنـدي تخبـل، و عنـدة مـسدس...

KEV: Everyone needs to shut up.

MUSA: *(Arabic) Be quiet!*

Suntteh!

صنطة !

> *Kev starts sporadically removing his gear. Helmet,*
> *shirt, eventually his pants come off.*

WOMAN: *(Arabic) What is he doing? Why is he doing that?*

Hathe shday-saw-wee? Hathe leysh hee-chee day-saw-wee?

هـاذة شـديـسوي؟ هـاذة لـيش هيـجي ديـسوي؟

KEV: *(to Tiger)* Bring it, Tiger. I'm right here, ready, bitch. Don't need no Kevlar, no flak, fuckin-A, just me and you. Me and you Tiger, I'm ready. *I'm ready!*

KEV: *(he starts to cry)* I did it once, I can do it again . . . I can kill him again . . .

MUSA: No. No killing.
The gun. Give it to me.

KEV: I didn't want to do it.

MUSA: I know. Here. Give it to me . . .
Yes. Yes. Yes.

> *Musa slowly takes the gun from Kev.*
>
> *Kev starts sobbing and collapses.*
>
> *The woman gets up and starts screaming at him,*
> *throwing the discarded blankets at him.*

WOMAN: *(Arabic) Nothing, you've got nothing, you're crazy, empty,*
soulless fools, all of you, ruining our lives with your stupid, mindless game!

Ente La shai', kulshee ma I'ndek, inte mejnoon, farigh, kulkum,
demertoo haeyatne b gheba'kum oo lu'abkum il ashwa'i-yeh

انت لا شيء، كـلشي مـا عنـدك، انـت مجنـون، فـارغ، مـا
عنـدك رحمة، كـلكم،دمـرتـو حيـاتـنة بـعبـائـكم و لـعبـكم
الـعشـوائـية !

KEV: I'm sorry! I'm sorry! I'm sorry!

WOMAN: *(Arabic)* *You! Where are you going?*

Ente! weyn rayih?

انت! وين رايح؟

MUSA: *(Arabic)* *I'm leaving.*

Ani rah-arooh.

انـي رح اروح.

Musa looks at the gold gun and then puts it in his pants and starts to leave.

WOMAN: *(Arabic)* *You're stealing, just like them! Stealing, a common thief!*

Ente det-boog, mithilhum, haramee, haramee a'adee!

انـتة دتـبوك، عيـنا مـثلهم! حرامـي، حرامـي عـادي!

MUSA: *(Arabic)* *Leave me alone.*

Joozee minnee.

جوزي مـني

Musa exits.

WOMAN: *(Arabic)* *Go! Go home you traitor, you thief!*

Rooh, rooh ilbaitek ya kha'in, ya haramee!

روح! روح الـبيـتك يـا خـائـن، يـا حرامـي!

MUSA: *(Arabic)* *This does not belong to him . . .*
This does not belong to him.

Hathe moo melthe!

هـاذة مـو مـالـتة!

MAN: *(Arabic)* *Would you tell me what's happening! Will you stop shouting, for God's sake?*

Met gooleelee hi shdayseer! Tigdereen tbettileen syah, il khattir alle?

متـكولـيلـي هـاي شديـصير! تـكدريـن تـبطلين صيـاح،
الـخـاطر الله؟

خـاطر الله؟

The woman looks at Kev, now half-buried under
blankets.

KEV: I'm sorry . . . I'm sorry . . . I'm just gonna stand here . . . I'm just
gonna stand here standing guard. Sir, yes sir . . . Sir, yes . . . sir . . .
I'm sorry!
Man down! Man down! Man attacked by . . . Man attacked by . . .
Man attacked.

WOMAN: *(quietly to her husband, Arabic) He's on the ground. He's crazy.*
He's sick. Come . . . come, we'll leave . . .

Hoo-eh al ga'. Hathe mejnoon. Hathe merreedh. Te'al . . . Te'al, khelee
en-rooh . . .

هوة عل كع . هـاذة مجنـون . هـاذة مـريض. تـعـال تـعـال،
خـلـي نـروح . . . . . .

(Woman and Man begin to exit; to Kev, Arabic) Go to hell! Leave us alone
and go to hell!

Rooh el-je-hen-nem! jooz min edne oo rooh el-je-hen-nem!

روح الجهنم ! جوز من عدنة و روح الجهنم !

Woman and Man exit. Kev huddles in the corner,
covering himself with blankets.

KEV: I'm sorry, I'm sorry! I'm just gonna stand here standing guard.
I shot him Tommy! I shot him! I fucking shot him, he's dead
Tommy!

Tiger looks at him. Lights illuminate a garden in
Baghdad. The garden is filled with large topiary
animals, carved out of hedges, but they are ruined,
burned and skeletal.

Bombs go off in the distance. Tiger examines the
topiary.

Scene 4.

> *Tiger, anxious, terrified, wanders the garden of topiary. The bombs in the distance cease. He looks around at the garden.*

TIGER: *(trying to pretend he's not scared)* It would have been better to have died young.

I'm an old ghost!

There's a gang of teenage rhesus monkeys down at the zoo who got blown up by an IED, and they're carrying on like a bunch of morons, milking the afterlife for all it's worth.

You want my advice? Die young, die with your friends.

It's the way to go.

(referring to topiary) I mean, what the fuck is this supposed to be? Animals made out of plants? Vegetative beasts? I've been walking around this city for days now, taking it all in, and nothing was very much of a surprise until I wandered into this garden here.

I mean . . . Who *does* this?

People. First they throw all the animals in a zoo and then they carve up the bushes to make it look like we never left.

Insult to injury. Insult to injury.

> *Bombs go off in the distance. Tiger cringes behind a hedge. The bombs cease.*

TIGER: I don't know why I'm so scared. You figure getting killed might be the last bad thing that can happen. The worst thing. I'll tell you right now: it's not the worst thing.

See, all my life, I've been plagued, as most tigers are, by this existential quandary: *Why am I here?* But now . . . I'm dead, I'm a ghost . . . and it's: *Why aren't I gone?*

I figured everything just ended. I figured the Leos . . . just ended. The suicidal polar bear . . . bones and dust.

It's alarming, this *life* after death.

The fact is, tigers are atheists. All of us. Unabashed. So, why am I still kicking around? Why me? Why here?

It doesn't seem fair. A dead cat consigned to this burning city doesn't seem just.

But here I am.

Dante in Hades. A Bengal tiger in Baghdad.

(beat) You didn't think I knew Dante, did you?

Now that I'm dead, I'm having all sorts of revelations about the world and existence. Things just appear to me. Knowledge, the stuff of the universe, it just sort of floats into me . . . Or maybe I'm floating into *it*.

But it doesn't help. No matter how much I learn, I'm still trapped. I just thought I'd be gone by now.

Why aren't I gone? Will someone please tell me why I'm not gone from here!?

> *Far off in the distance, the Muslim call to prayer is still heard. Tiger listens to it.*

TIGER: You hear that? That call to prayer? A constellation of minarets surrounds this garden, each one singing in a different key. They come in like a fog, five times a day. Different mosques, all over the city, calling out to God, voices intermingling in the air.

When an atheist suddenly finds himself walking around after death, he has got some serious reevaluating to do.

> *The call to prayer continues.*

TIGER: Listen!

Calling out to God in this mess.

God.

Can you believe it?

> *A loud bomb goes off and Tiger instinctively covers himself with his arms, and then looks skyward.*

Scene 5.

Kev lies on a hospital bed.

Tom enters.

KEV: Tommy?

TOM: Hey. What's up.

KEV: You're back.

TOM: I came back.
   Check it out. Bionic hand.

KEV: Holy shit.

TOM: They do you up right. I'm like Robocop.

KEV: Why'd you come back?

TOM: Didn't want to go out like that.
   Besides, I had stuff I needed to get.

KEV: Like your toilet seat?

TOM: Yeah, that's one thing. And my gun.

KEV: Let me see your hand.

TOM: Check it out.

KEV: That's badass.

TOM: Yeah.

KEV: They've had me in here like a week now.

TOM: What happened?

KEV: It was fucked up.

TOM: Yeah?

KEV: We were doing these night raids? And I went around the back
and booked it upstairs? I go in this room, this motherfucker comes out
from under the bed. Clocked me in the face. I was out. Next thing I
know, I'm on my way here.

I wanna get back, you know? This is bullshit. But they keep running tests. They keep telling me they're running tests.

TOM: Yeah.

KEV: How was America.

TOM: It was all right.

KEV: You get any Mickey D's?

TOM: Yeah, I got some. Right before I came back.

KEV: What'd you get?

TOM: What did I order?

KEV: Yeah, at Mickey D's.

TOM: I don't know. Big Mac.

KEV: Big Mac combo?

TOM: Yeah. With the fries and Coke.

KEV: I always get McChicken combo.

TOM: Yeah, that's good, too.

KEV: What else you do there.

TOM: I don't know. Got this.

KEV: You get your dick wet?

TOM: No, man.

KEV: You didn't? All the way back to the States and you didn't? You even see any bitches back there?

TOM: Yeah, sure. At the hospital. My nurse.

KEV: You tap that?

TOM: No, man.

KEV: You didn't tap that?

TOM: No, man, Jesus. I got surgery for my hand, okay? I wasn't thinking about getting laid.

KEV: I wish I could get some pussy.

TOM: Yeah. Sure.

Long pause.

KEV: You know that tiger?

TOM: Yeah.

KEV: I shot him with your gold gun.

TOM: Yeah, I know. I was there. Remember?

KEV: I'm just saying.

TOM: You have it?

KEV: What?

TOM: The gold gun, do you have it?

KEV: Not with me.

TOM: Not with you?

KEV: I told you, man. I'm out on a fucking night raid, next thing I know I'm on my way here. It's not like I had time to pack, you know what I'm saying?

TOM: Where's the gun?

KEV: Somewhere safe.

TOM: Where?

KEV: I don't know man, where's your toilet seat?

TOM: None of your business, Kev. Where's my gold gun?

KEV: You know what, man? I saved you. Okay? I saved your life.

TOM: I don't care what you did, where's my gun?

KEV: It's in your momma's ass.

TOM: What?

KEV: I said, your gun? It's shoved up your mother's ass. She put it there herself.

TOM: Kev. Do you know that my mother is dead?

KEV: She is?

TOM: Yeah.

KEV: Aw shit man, I'm sorry, I didn't mean to go off on the moms. I was just saying, you know? I thought you came to visit me and see how I was doing and catch up and everything.

TOM: The gun is mine. I want it back.

KEV: You got your toilet seat! That's gotta be worth way more.

TOM: We're not gonna argue about this.

KEV: You should just give it to me. Be a decent fucking guy, you know? I killed a tiger with it.
   Tom sticks his prosthetic hand in Kev's face.

TOM: Look at this. Look at this, motherfucker!

KEV: What? God, what's your problem?

TOM: I lost my hand! It's gone, do you get that, asshole?

KEV: Yeah, I know, I can see! I was there!

TOM: I was gonna go home and work for my uncle. What am I supposed to do now? I lost my right hand!

KEV: Dude, that thing is top of the line. You're like Robocop.

TOM: No I'm not. I'm a stupid handicapped jerk. I didn't even get a Purple Heart.

KEV: That sucks.

TOM: Yeah, that sucks. So I got some gold that I can get and so maybe I have a fucking livelihood when I get back.

KEV: A livelihood?

TOM: Yeah, that's like what the meaning of your life is.

KEV: So what, your livelihood's gonna be having a gold toilet seat and a gold gun?

TOM: No . . .

KEV: Cause that sounds like kind of a wack-ass livelihood, you know?

TOM: Just shut the fuck up about it.

KEV: Tommy, you ever think about him?

TOM: Who?

KEV: The tiger.

TOM: He *bit off my hand.*

KEV: You ever see him?

TOM: What?

KEV: You ever see the tiger? Like just hanging around?

TOM: . . . The tiger.

KEV: Yeah. Or talking.

TOM: What are you talking about?

KEV: I'm asking you a question!

TOM: Yeah, what? What is your question?

KEV: I'm asking you!

TOM: What?!

KEV: I'm asking you, you ever see that tiger around or anything?

TOM: The tiger is dead.

> *Tiger enters, sees them, but hangs back, doing his own thing.*

KEV: I know the tiger is dead, I killed the fucking tiger. I'm asking you if you ever seen him. Like his ghost.

TOM: No, Kev. I've never seen the tiger's *ghost.* I don't believe in ghosts. Especially I don't believe in animal ghosts.

KEV: I got to tell you something, man.

TOM: Jesus. This is why everyone hates you, Kev. Cause you're a fucking idiot.

KEV: Seriously, man, can I tell you something? You're like the only person I can tell this stuff to.

TOM: I don't even really *know* you, man.

KEV: Can I just tell you something? Please?

TOM: Fine.

KEV: I mean I'm trying to tell you something!

TOM: I said fine! Okay!

KEV: Trying to be like a normal guy, you know? Trying to tell you something. Something wack. Something kind of wack, okay?

TOM: Would you just tell me?

KEV: Okay.
   (beat) So look. You know I said I was on that night raid?

TOM: Yeah. And the dude came out from under the bed and whacked you upside the head. I know.

KEV: Okay, so I'm like lying there, right? And the dude takes off, right? So I'm alone in the bedroom.

TOM: You're alone in the bedroom.

KEV: And the ghost of that tiger walked into the room . . .

TOM: The ghost of the tiger . . .

KEV: I'm telling you, man, it was crazy. But he wasn't like how he was in real life. He was, like, walking on his hind legs.

TOM: No shit. His hind legs.

KEV: Yeah, and he could talk!

TOM: He could talk, what did he say?

KEV: He started babbling all this bullshit to me, and then I fainted.

TOM: You fainted?

KEV: Yeah man, I mean I was freaking out.

TOM: And then what?

KEV: That's the thing. I don't remember much after that.

TOM: That's a pretty stupid fucking story.

KEV: You're not listening to me!

TOM: What?

KEV: I didn't finish yet!

TOM: Well then finish!

Kev gathers himself.

KEV: . . . Trying to tell a story here . . .

TOM: Tell the story or I'm leaving.

KEV: Forget it.

TOM: Forget it. Jesus you are retarded, you know that?
Where's the gun, Kev?

KEV: I thought you came to see me.

TOM: Well, I didn't come to see you, Kev. What am I, your mother?

KEV: Dude, my mom is dead.

TOM: No she's not.

KEV: So?

TOM: Oh my God! You have got to be the dumbest piece of shit in the entire fucking world.

KEV: Whatever, man! Did you even get the letter I sent you?

Beat.

TOM: Yeah. I got the letter.

KEV: I wrote you a fucking letter, dude.

TOM: I know, I . . .
Thanks.
Thanks for the letter you sent me.

KEV: You got it?

TOM: Yeah. I got it right after my first surgery.

KEV: Yeah, I'm good at writing letters and shit.

TOM: I didn't ask you to write me.

KEV: I know you didn't. I ain't no faggot.

TOM: I didn't say you were.

KEV: I wrote you a letter, man! I mean, I saw what happened to you. Do you even remember? Do you even remember that tiger biting your hand off?

TOM: I remember enough.

KEV: Well, fuckin-A! That was some crazy shit! I don't exactly think that's like normal. Even for war and shit.
I just . . .
I felt bad, you know? For you, I mean.
I was glad to kill that tiger. I was glad I got to save your life, Tommy.
You're my good buddy. That's what people do when they have a friend and shit.

TOM: Well, thanks.

KEV: Don't mention it.
We're partners, you know? We been through battle together, Tommy.

TOM: Do you know where you *are*, Kev?

KEV: The *war*, man.

TOM: No, I mean here.

KEV: Hospital.

TOM: They think you're crazy.

KEV: I ain't crazy.

TOM: You weren't attacked by no Iraqi from under the bed either.

KEV: You weren't even there.

TOM: You're going nuts.

KEV: No man, I'm cool.

TOM: Gulf War Syndrome, you little bitch.

KEV: I do not!

TOM: You are fucked, man.

KEV: You don't really have a great bedside manner, you know what I'm saying Tommy?

TOM: They got you on suicide watch.

KEV: That's not true.

TOM: Yeah they do.

KEV: Bullshit, man! If they did, they wouldn't be leaving sharp objects and shit around, you know? They wouldn't leave sharp objects around my bed for me to find!

TOM: What are you talking about?

KEV: I'm talking about the tiger!

TOM: The tiger is *dead*!

KEV: He's not, Tommy. He's right here.

TOM: Where.

KEV: Here. In this room. He hangs out here all the time. He's here right now, Tommy.

> Tom starts to leave.

KEV: (*starts to cry*) Tommy. Don't leave.
You're my best friend.

TOM: I am not your friend.

KEV: Yes you are. You are, man. And I need you, okay? I'm so scared. He's everywhere, you know? Everywhere I look is that stupid fucking tiger.

TOM: Well, that's your psycho problem, Kev. Not mine.
Now, I have some gold left that I have to get before I leave

here and if I don't get the gun back from you, I'm gonna kill you. Understand?

> *Tom exits.*

> *Tiger stands near Kev.*

KEV: Aw shit, man.

TIGER: Nice guy.

KEV: Shut up.

TIGER: I just remembered something: sixteen years ago I killed two children.
  A little girl and a little boy. Sister and brother.

KEV: Fucking dead-ass ghost motherfucker.
  Just hanging around, trying to make everyone think I'm some crazy-ass piece-of-shit soldier.

TIGER: This was back in the Sunderbans, in West Bengal.
  Home! The only place these crazy stripes actually camouflage me.

KEV: I'm sorry! Okay? I'm sorry I shot you!

TIGER: I'm telling you, for the most part, I'm very shy! I like to sit back and wait for something to walk by so I can kill it and eat it. I'm a simple guy with simple tastes.

KEV: You know what, man? I wrote my brother about you. He said you're just a figment of my imagination and shit. He said you were just one of those fucked-up things about being in war. So what's up now? You don't even exist, bitch! Except for me! Except for me.

TIGER: Anyhow, the two children had strayed away from their village. The girl was collecting wood or something. I watched them curve around a corner. I was absolutely still. The little boy, at one point, turned and looked directly at me, into my eyes. But he didn't register the significance. He never did.

KEV: You know what though? Fuck Tommy. My brother is a hundred times better than Tommy. If I was on suicide watch, then they wouldn't've left shit behind that I could . . . you know, shit like this?

Kev lifts his mattress up and takes out a large, sharp piece of metal, like an old knife or scrap metal.

KEV: Shit like this!

TIGER: I was hungry. They were food.

KEV: If you don't get the fuck out of my head, bitch, I will kill us both. Don't think I won't do it. I killed you once, I'll kill you again!

TIGER: And I caused untold misery to the parents of those children. But what could I do? I'm a tiger.

KEV: Get. Out. Of. My. Head!

TIGER: It wasn't cruel. It was lunch!
A basic primordial impulse isn't cruel!
But here's what I'm wondering:
What if it *is*?
What if my every meal has been an act of cruelty? What if my very nature is in direct conflict with the moral code of the universe? That would make me a fairly damned individual.
After all, *lunch* usually consists of the weak, the small, the stupid, the young, the crippled. Because they're easier to kill.

KEV: You want my hand? You want to eat my hand, just like you did Tommy? Here! Maybe then you'll leave me alone, just like you leave Tommy alone!

Kev starts cutting his wrist. Trying not so much to slit his wrist, as to actually cut his hand off.

TIGER: I'm guilty! That's why I'm stuck here. I'm being punished.
But you'd think the twelve years in a zoo, caged, never hunting, never killing, never breaking God's ridiculous *law* . . . you'd think I would have atoned for my tigerness. But maybe that's my way out of here. Assuming God exists, and assuming this punishment has a reason, I have to atone. I need you tell me: How do I do it?

KEV: Eat it, take it. Eat my fucking hand, I don't want it!

TIGER: I don't want your hand. I want your help.

KEV: I'll get a new one like Tommy. Fucking Robocop and everything.
See? I can still do what I want. I can do whatever . . . whatever I
want and no faggot-ass tiger is gonna . . . is gonna . . .
Yeah.

> *Kev dies, and crumples in a heap on the bed.*

> *Tiger goes to Kev, looks him over.*

TIGER: *(realizing)* Shit.
I bite off the one kid's hand. And then I drive this one to suicide.

> *Tiger shakes his head. Looks at the topiary head
> and then starts to walk out, defeated.*

TIGER: *(to audience)* I am digging myself into one hell of a fucking hole.

> *Tiger exits.*

Scene 6.

> *Musa sits at a table in his home. He looks exhausted
> and depressed. He holds the gold gun and stares at
> it, toying with it, sometimes aiming it, sometimes
> stroking it.*

> *The front door opens. Uday Hussein enters carrying
> the severed head of his brother, Qusay. Uday is
> riddled with bullet holes. Otherwise, he seems fine.*

> *Uday is joyously psychotic. He is delighted by just
> about everything. However, he should never laugh
> maniacally.*

UDAY: Knock! Knock!

> *Musa looks up, but does not respond.*

UDAY: I said, Knock! Knock! You are to answer "Who is there?"

Beat. Uday speaks sometimes to the head of his
brother, sometimes to Musa.

UDAY: He's no fun today! You're no fun today!
(beat) Fine, I will say! "Who is there?"
"Knock! Knock!"
"Who is there?"
"Uday and Qusay!"
"Uday and Qusay *who*?"

> *Uday walks up to the table where Musa sits, puts his*
> *hands on the table, and bends down so he is nose to*
> *nose with Musa.*

UDAY: Uday and Qusay *Hussein*, motherfucker!
(beat) Look Qusay! It is Mansour. My trusted gardener. But he is
not keeping the land any longer.
He has a gun! Qusay, he has a gun!

> *Uday looks at the gun more carefully.*

UDAY: Well, what is *this*? Qusay! This is *my* gun! It is my gold-plated
semiautomatic pistol. Crafted in Riyadh! Qusay, isn't that remarkable?

> *Uday puts Qusay's face to his ear, as if Qusay were*
> *whispering to him.*

UDAY: Qusay says you are a cockroach piece of mothershit worth zero
weight in gold. Qusay, his English is not as good as my own. But I like
this, I like this *piece of mothershit,* because that is what you are, you
piece of mothershit peasant.

> *Musa points the gun in Uday's face.*

UDAY: It is not polite, when you have guests, to shove a gun in their
face. I imagine you know this, and so the sting is all the worse. I do not
like rudeness.

MUSA: Allahu Akbar.

UDAY: *(with fury)* Shut up!

> *Uday walks around the table, behind Musa, and sticks the gun to the back of Musa's head.*

UDAY: How does this feel? How does it feel to have this beautiful weapon pressed against your worthless skull? Qusay! Should I shoot this peasant?

> *Qusay nods.*

UDAY: *(loud, joyous, about to shoot)* Fine! Thank you for claiming my gun!
Thank you!
Thank you!
Thank you!

MUSA: *(Arabic)* No please! Don't kill me! Please don't kill me! Please!

La' reja'en! Le tuktulnee! Reja'en le tuktulnee! Reja'en!

لاء رجاء! لا تـكتـلـني! رجاء لا تـكتـلـني! رجاء!

> *Uday takes the gun away from Musa's head.*

UDAY: *(cheerful)* Okay okay okay okay okay.

> *Uday walks around, suddenly in a very reflective mood.*

UDAY: I went looking for my brother after they killed me. All I found was his head. How do you like that?
Poor Qusay. I wonder if he's walking around with my head.
That would be funny.
I find all this very funny, Mansour. Funny, funny, funny.

> *Uday pulls up a chair and sits at the table, across from Musa. He smokes and kicks up his feet on the table.*

UDAY: *(truly aggrieved)* But people don't like me. They say I am a bad man. Evil. A torturer. They say I tortured people.

(beat) Of course I fucking tortured people.

When you have people who have wronged you, who have attempted to kill you or your father or your brother, or you have people who look lasciviously upon your wife or your sisters or your girlfriend, and these men have felt it in their hearts that they would kill you and would wipe everything that has become you off the face of the earth, let me tell you, my friend, you would torture them.

> *Uday speaks with great relish, as if it were a great joke, or as if describing a delicious and wonderful recipe.*

UDAY: You would . . .

Tie them up . . . and you would beat the soles of their feet with wet bamboo until they couldn't walk. And then you'd watch them stumble around the room, trying to walk on the bloody soles of their stupid feet.

And then you'd laugh and break their ribs.

And you'd pull out their teeth and their toenails and then watch them try to run away again.

This is better than any movie you've ever seen!

And then once they have tired of this, and they have given themselves up to you, ready for death, then you deny them this death and you bring in *their* women. And you have your way with them. Because to watch your wife get fucked by a man who is about to kill you, well, that is a piece-of-shit day you are having, my friend. *And that is why you don't ever fuck with Uday Hussein!*

> *Uday leans forward, looking at Musa intently.*

UDAY: Knock! Knock! Anyone home? I just told a funny joke and you don't laugh and you don't speak to me and you are very rude, Mansour. Very rude.

> *Uday kicks back again, soliloquizing.*

UDAY: But, yeah man, I am dead. I got about twenty-six bullets from here to here on me.

The Americans got me.

Me and Qusay. And then what do they do? These U.S. Fucking Troops? What do they do? They come into my home and they steal everything I have, like common little thieves. Like piranhas.

I *had* piranhas. I would know.

And it is these hungry, greedy little Americans, who you work for. You work for them to kill us. To steal our oil. To fuck us in the ass, Mansour.

MUSA: No.

UDAY: *No?*

MUSA: I do not work for the Americans.

UDAY: You can lie to me, Mansour, but you cannot expect me to lap up your shit like the dogs you work for. *You*, Mansour: a traitor in everyone's midst. Watch your step. One false move and kaput.

MUSA: I am a different person now.

UDAY: No, piece of mothershit. You are the same. And you are lying to everyone who wants to trust you. You steal from the Americans and you steal from me. And you lie, Mansour.

You lie to me.

MUSA: I do not lie.

UDAY: You lie! Why do you lie to me!?

You are thinking you can slip one past me?

Who am I?

MUSA: You are dead.

UDAY: Yes! I am dead! And yet, here I am . . . roaming around Baghdad. Uday Hussein will not go away, Mansour. He is not so simply shot down by a bunch of teenage Ronald McDonalds who think they are the hot shit of 2003. Americans! Always thinking that when things die, they go away.

Uday smokes and offers a cigar to Musa.

UDAY: Smoke?

MUSA: No thank you.

UDAY: It's a Cuban!

(re: the good cigar) Cubans.

Fuck me, man. Fuck me in the ass.

Breathe it in. Even a dead man loves a Cuban.

(beat) I'm doing good things here, Mansour. My pure existence causes destruction.

Everything going down in the streets? The war still being fought? What they call the insurrection?

I am the insurrection, Mansour. It is me.

(beat) You're not impressed? Oh, what's wrong, Mansour? Are you still mad about that little thing between us?

> *Musa doesn't answer.*

UDAY: I bet you are. I bet you are angry with Uday. But you work for me, and so I have rights, and your little sister . . .

Little Hadia . . . she works for me too.

> *Musa, breathing heavily, suddenly screams, jumps to his feet, kicking the table, and finally collapses on the floor.*

UDAY: Okay, good. Yeah, crybaby. You can go and cry like a baby.

MUSA: What do you want.

UDAY: What do I want? What do I want?

But that is not the question, Mansour. The question is what do *you* want? You find yourself in a fucked-up situation all of a sudden, my friend.

> *Uday holds the gold gun out in front of them.*

UDAY: This gun was a gift to me from a Saudi sheikh, I can't even remember his name.

They're all faggots, the Saudis. You know?

He gave me this thing and, man, it was the best thing I ever got in my life.

That's when I started having everything turned into gold. All my guns, kitchenware, tools, my bedposts, my toothbrush, even the toilet, sahib. Shitting on gold, man! That is the king's way, I am telling you!

MUSA: *(quietly)* King Midas.

UDAY: What?

MUSA: *(quietly)* Nothing.

UDAY: What did you say? *(beat)*
    You said "King Midas" is that what you said?
    (beat) And then you say, never mind, because me, Uday Hussein, doesn't know who King Midas is? Because me, Uday Hussein, educated in Switzerland, doesn't know about Greek mythology, but you, little peasant from Baghdad, is knowing more than me?

>   *Uday grabs Musa by the hair, pulling his head back.*

UDAY: The Midas touch! You think I am like Midas? No no, my man, I am better than him, because I don't need magical powers, because I don't need them. And then if I had them, how would I be able to do this?

>   *Uday grabs Musa by the hair and slams his face into the desk. Musa falls to the ground.*

UDAY: And this!

>   *Uday kicks Musa in the stomach and then spits on him.*

UDAY: You think I want to transform shit like you into gold? Is that what you think, Mansour?

MUSA: . . . No . . .

UDAY: No! Absolutely right. No.

>   *Uday picks up the gold gun.*

UDAY: You take this back, Mansour. And you know those stupid kid Americans who stole it, they are criminals, just like everyone else.

They want it back, but now you have it. So you know what you have now? You have some leverage!

>*Musa looks at the gun and then back at Uday.*

MUSA: I won't do anything for you.

UDAY: Oh but it's not *for me*, Mansour. I'm here, but I don't need anything. I have you. I have Qusay's head, I have Iraq, just as I always have. And I'm never going to go away.

Look at me.

What are you going to do with your life? Where are you going to get work as a gardener? There's nothing left to garden, my man. And you think the Americans are going to employ you forever? They're already retreating. And they're going to leave you here with nothing green and nothing to work with except a big pile of shit.

The only thing you have is me and my gun.

>*Uday gives the gun to Musa. Musa takes it.*
>
>*Uday grabs Qusay's head and listens, as if Qusay is whispering to him.*
>
>*Uday laughs at Qusay's wit.*

UDAY: Qusay is funny.

He remembers your sister, too. Hadia. Haadeeeaaahhh.

Do you know what the thing about your sister was that we loved?

>*Musa drops his head in defeat. He begins to choke with grief.*

UDAY: Mansour. Look at me.

Do you know what was interesting about her? The way she quivered, Mansour.

She was like one of those sculptures you were doing in my garden.

What did you call those animals you made?

What is that called, Mansour? You tell me, but I am always forgetting.

MUSA: Topiary.

UDAY: Topiary! I love this topiary! You are the real artist, you know that Mansour?

(seeing Musa's grief) What? What do you want, you *brought her to my garden!*

You brought your little virgin sister to *me!*

I take what is mine, boss. I take it.

And you should have heard her.

Such a little creature make such a great noise.

What a mess that was, my man.

Maybe someday you can make a topiary out of your sister. You can carve her out of the hedges. And she can quiver in the wind.

You need to start working again, Mansour.

All your animals have died.

Uday exits, leaving Musa with the gun.

ACT 2
Scene 1.

Tiger appears.

TIGER: This place is lousy with ghosts.

And the new ones are irritating. They're walking around, wide-eyed . . . *What happened to me? Where am I?*

You're dead and you're in Baghdad. Shut up.

Anyhow, the other day, I'm walking down the street. The street is literally *on fire.*

And I see this little girl. Her life is like a soap bubble, and then pop! She's here, in the middle of the street, looking up at me. And she says to me: What are you? And I tell her, I'm a tiger.

She asks me am I going to eat her.

And I say, no, I gave up eating children.

She says why?

And I say, I don't know, it's this philosophy I'm working out about sin and redemption since God is apparently nuts.

And the girl just kind of looks at me.

And I'm like, think about it, if God's watching, why'd he snuff you out? Why are you standing here, alone, in a burning street, with a dead tiger?

Why is half your face gone?

And she says yeah, but why'd you give up eating children?

And I tell her the bit about the two kids in the forest, and how I keep thinking about them and how I have all this guilt.

She doesn't understand that. The guilt thing. She doesn't have any guilt. And I'm like, of course you don't. What did you ever do? Nothing.

She tells me she's afraid.

I tell her I am too.

Which you'd think would be comforting, given the circumstances, but somehow, being blown to bits and then coming face-to-face with the likes of *me* . . .

Well the girl starts to cry, you know?

Her one eye cries.

And I say, don't cry. But she cries harder. And so I say to her, hey do you want to see something? And she stops crying for a second. And she's like, what?

And I say it's a . . . I tell her it's a garden.

And she looks at me as if to say, big fucking deal, like I haven't seen a garden before?

And I say, no it's a special garden.

Lights up on the topiary animals.

And I don't know why I say this, but I say, it's God's garden.

I tell her it's God's garden.

He likes gardens, see. He tests us in them, he tempts us in them, he builds them up and tears them apart. It's like his fucking hobby.

And she's skeptical, I can see that, but I bring her here and she sees these plants, these animals, and she's never seen anything like them. And I nailed it because she's not crying anymore. She's walking around the garden, pointing. *A lion! A camel! An elephant!*

Fucking kids, you know?

And I mean, this whole time I'm talking out of my ass, this business about God's garden, etcetera. Maybe she knows I'm bullshitting, too. The girl is no dummy, even if she does only have half a brain.

But for a second we both look up at these ruined shrubs and think, okay Man, You work in Mysterious Ways. We get it.

And I feel this swell of hope.

And then she turns to me and she's like, *When will He get here?*
What?

She says, *When will God get here? If this is His garden, then He has to come to it, He has to tend to it.*

Look! she says. *The green is all burned.*

This animal has lost his head.

Well?!

What am I supposed to tell her?

I'm asking You to tell me.

Because if You don't . . . I'm going to have to watch her cry again. I'm gonna have to sit here and watch that little single eye of hers well up with tears . . .

Until eventually she'll stop. She'll stop crying.

And her brain will fill up, as mine did, and she'll understand the universe.

And her spirit or body or whatever You've left us with, it will go on to other things.

And this moment, *this fucking moment* when she appraises a ruined piece of beauty with her one good eye, *this moment* will become extinct.

Just like You.

Is that what You *want? Say something! This animal has lost her head!* Speak through me, or through her, or through someone, but speak, God, speak!

> *A back room in a converted officers' building.*
>
> *Tom sits at a chair. Across the room a teenage Iraqi girl sits.*
>
> *She wears a hijab head scarf, but a tight T-shirt and blue jeans.*
>
> *They don't look at each other. Tom stares at the floor.*

Tom gets up and paces around the room, nervous.

Tom looks out the door, anxious, waiting for someone.

GIRL: Ficky-fick.

TOM: Yeah. Ficky-fick.

GIRL: Ficky-fick!

TOM: *(loudly, as if volume could translate)* Just . . . five minutes . . .

The girl is irritated, shakes her head dismissively at him.

Tom sits back down. Kev enters. He holds his own severed hand.

Tom doesn't look at Kev, but senses him and shakes his head in frustration.

KEV: Dear Tommy,
How are you. I am fine.

TOM: *(quietly)* Leave me alone.

GIRL: *(irritated)* Ficky-fick, eh?

TOM: Yeah, ficky-fick! Five minutes! Would you just wait!?

Girl, not intimidated, shakes her head dismissively.

KEV: I don't know why I did it, Tommy. I was trying to chop off my hand and give it to the tiger. But it's a pretty intense process to remove your own hand.

TOM: *(squeezes hands over his ears)* Go away. Just get outta here.

GIRL: *(Arabic) For twenty dollars we can have sex.*

B'ishreen dolar a-nam weyak.

بـعشريـن دولار انـام ويـاك.

Ficky-fick! Ficky-fick!

TOM: I'm not talking to you! Shut up!
(points to his watch) Five minutes!

KEV: *(shows his hand)* First, you have to crack and break the bone. Bones, actually. There's a lot of them. On the proximal side, the scaphoid, lunate, triquetrum and pisiform. On the distal side, trapezoid, capitate, and hamate.

I couldn't fracture all of them. They're hard. And I only partially shredded my volar radiocarpal ligament.

These things keep us together, you know? I never knew about this stuff before. But now I do. I am understanding how things relate.

> *Tom looks at his prosthetic hand. He looks at the girl, and then shifts away from both the girl and Kev, seemingly embarrassed of his hand.*

> *Kev gets up and starts to leave.*

KEV: I'm just saying, Tommy, think about the physiology of the wrist! We are put together so well! And that tiger tore off your hand in about two seconds! With just his mouth! How strong his jaws must be! How hungry he must have been! He just took it off and ate it.

It's amazing, how quickly you can lose a part of yourself.

I am glad I met you because you are a true friend.

Your friend, Kev.

TOM: *(jumping up, shouting) I'm not your friend! Leave me alone!*

> *The girl is startled.*

> *Kev exits, Musa enters, rushed.*

> *Musa looks sick, exhausted.*

TOM: What the fuck man?

MUSA: I'm so sorry . . . I'm . . .

TOM: Well, get the fuck in here!
Okay. I'm sorry I shouted. Will you tell her I'm sorry I shouted?

MUSA: Who is this girl?

TOM: She's a girl.

MUSA: I can see that. Who is she?

TOM: I just need you to translate.

MUSA: You told me this was for . . .

TOM: Never mind what I told you. Will you just translate?

MUSA: Translate what?

TOM: Tell her I'm sorry I shouted.

MUSA: *(Arabic) He is sorry he shouted.*

Hoo-e mita'siff ala syaha.

هوه متاسف عله صياحه.

Girl is not impressed.

Musa looks at Tom. Tom looks back at both of them.

TOM: Okay. Can we take care of this?

MUSA: Take care of what? You told me we were conducting interviews.

TOM: Just translate.

MUSA: To her? To a girl? I'm not that kind of translator.

TOM: What if I take this to your RSO? I give you a directive, you follow it, or they will kick your ass to the curb, Habib. Do your fucking job.
 (to Girl) Ficky-fick.

GIRL: Ficky-fick.

TOM: Yeah.
 (to Musa) Ficky-fick?

MUSA: What are you talking about?

GIRL: Yeah. Ficky-fick.

TOM: So check it out.
 I been whacking off since I was eleven.

Always with the right hand. Probably at least twice a day since I was eleven, always with the right hand.

That's a lot of whacking off.

I didn't think about it.

My name's Tom.

GIRL: Ficky-fick.

TOM: Yeah. Ficky-fick.

It's not the same with the left hand.

I broke in my right hand after all those years of yanking it every day. It had the right shape.

It was familiar to me.

GIRL: Ficky-fick. Twenty dollar!

TOM: Tell her.

MUSA: Tell her what?

TOM: What I just said. Tell her.

MUSA: *(to Girl; Arabic) He will pay you. But he is shy and wants to talk a little bit first.*

Rah yidfa'lich. Bess hoo-eh mistihee u-yreed yihchee shway-eh o-el.

رح يـدفـعـلـج . بـس هـوه مـسـتـحـي و يـريـد يـحـجـي شـويـه اول .

TOM: Did you tell her?

MUSA: I did.

TOM: Does she understand?

MUSA: Probably not.

I don't understand.

TOM: It's because of the shape! And the angle. I don't know! It's just different.

And I can't get off. It's as simple as that.

MUSA: What exactly do you want me to tell her?

TOM: Tell her that!

MUSA: I did.

TOM: So?

MUSA: Even if what I told her made any sense, I'm not sure she understands what you want.

GIRL: *(Arabic) Does he have money with him?*

Inde floos weeyah?

عنده فلوس ويا؟

MUSA: *(Arabic) He has money and he will pay you.*

Inde floos oo rah yidfa'lich.

عنده فلوس و رح يدفعلج.

GIRL: *(Arabic) For twenty dollars we can have sex.*

B'ishreen dolar a-nam weya.

بعشرين دولار انام ويا.

MUSA: *(Arabic) He will give you what you want.*

Rah yidfa'lich ili treedee.

رح يدفعلج الى تريدي.

TOM: What are you guys babbling about?

MUSA: *(Arabic) He has a problem with his hand.*

Hoo-eh inde mushkilleh b'eedeh.

هوة عنده مشكلة بايدة.

GIRL: *(Arabic) What happened to him?*

Sh-sar bee?

شصار بي؟

TOM: *(angry)* You know that's very rude!
   I'm standing right here and you guys are fucking talking on and on like that! Especially since I just kind of revealed some personal stuff and everything.

GIRL: *(Arabic) What does he want to do?*

Shee-reed ysa-wee?

شــريــد يـــسوي؟

MUSA: She wants to know what you want.

TOM: What do I want?

MUSA: Yes.

TOM: I want her to stand behind me and whack me off with her right hand.

Musa stares at Tom.

TOM: Look I don't care what you think about it, Habib, you're here to translate. Translate. Save your fucking judgments for your own time.

MUSA: I'm just trying to figure out how to say this in Arabic.

TOM: Fucking tell her and then get out so I can do my business.

Musa slowly explains to the girl in Arabic, using gestures to aid his description.

MUSA: Okay . . .
(*Arabic*) *He wants you to stand behind him and reach around and use your hand on him so he has pleasure. He says he cannot do this anymore because he has lost his hand.*

Yireed-ich togfeen war-ah u-tmid-deen eedich al-*eh* hette twen-is-ee. Hoo-eh yigool inoo hoo-eh may-igder ysa-wee heechee il-nefseh ba'ad lee-en foo-ked eedeh.

يــريـدج تــوكفـيـن ورا و تمـديـن ايـدج عليـه حتى تـونـسي.
هوة يـكـول انـو هوة مـيـكـدر يـسوي هيـجي لــنفسه بـعـد لان
فقـد ايـدة .

GIRL: (*Arabic*) *For twenty dollars we can have sex.*

B'ishreen dolar a-nam weya

بـعشريـن دولار انـام ويـا .

MUSA: She said she will have sex with you for twenty dollars.

TOM: I don't want to have sex with her.
I'll pay her more. I'll pay her thirty.

MUSA: *(Arabic) For thirty dollars he wants you to stand behind him and reach around and use your hand on him. It is important to him because he has no hand.*

B-tlatheen dolar yireedich togfeen war-ah u-tmid-deen eedich oo testa'mileeheh al-*eh*. Hathe shee muhimm il-eh lee-en hooeh ma inde eed.

بـتلائـن دولار يـريـدج تـوكـفـتن وراه و تمـديـن ايـدج و تستعمليـها عـليـه . هـاذة شي مـهم الــه لان هوة مـا عنده ايـد .

GIRL: *(Arabic) What happened to his hand?*

Sh-sar b'eedeh?

شصار بـايـدة ؟

MUSA: She wants to know what happened to your hand.

TOM: I lost it.

MUSA: *(Arabic) He lost it.*

Foo-ked-heh.

فقـدهة .

GIRL: *(Arabic) How?*

Shlone?

شلـون ؟

MUSA: How?

TOM: In battle. In fucking battle, okay? I'm fighting in a war here and I got my hand blowed off and now I can't even jack off right. So tell her to get behind me and start me up. *Now.* Because I'm sick of this shit.

MUSA: *(Arabic)* . . . *war.*

. . . harrub.

فقـد ايـدة بـالحرب .

GIRL: *(Arabic) Can I see his hand?*

Igder ashoof eedeh?

اكـدر اشـوف ايـدة؟

MUSA: She wants to look at your hand.

Tom looks at the girl.

TOM: Why.

MUSA: She wants to see it.

Tom lifts and shows her his hand. She walks to him and looks at it.

TOM: Top of the line.

The girl holds Tom's hand, tapping it, inspecting it. As she touches his hand, Tom looks at her. Something about her touch seems to affect him.

TOM: It's not that hard. All she needs to do is stand behind me and then I can show her. I can help her do what she needs to do. It's easier than fucking. It's easier than ficky-fick.

GIRL: *(Arabic) This is shiny!*

Hathee tilma'!

هـاذي تـلـمـع !

TOM: What she say?

MUSA: *(Arabic) What?*

Shinoo?

شنـو؟

GIRL: *(Arabic) This is shiny!*

Hathee tilma'!

هـاذي تـلـمـع !

MUSA: *(exasperated at Girl and Tom)* She says your hand is shiny.

TOM: *(to Girl; loud, but not angry)* Yeah, it's shiny!

MUSA: If you can show her what to do, why do you need me here?
(beat) I am saying, you ask me to accompany you here and that it is very important, but it seems you don't need me really all that much.
(beat) It's just this crude act. It doesn't need to be explained.

TOM: I *needed to explain it.*

MUSA: Do you have any aspirin?

TOM: What?

MUSA: I have headache. Do you have medicine?

TOM: No.

GIRL: *(Arabic) Can this be removed?*

Hathee mumkin tinshal?

هـاذي ممكن تـنشـال؟

MUSA: *(Arabic) What?*

Shinoo?

شنـو؟

GIRL: *(Arabic) Can his hand come off?*

Yigder ytulle' eedeh?

يـكدر يـطلع ايـدة؟

TOM: What?

MUSA: She wants to know if it can come off. Your hand.

TOM: What are you talking about?

MUSA: She wants to know if you can *remove* the hand. If it is possible.

TOM: *(suddenly angry)* Why?! What difference does it make?!

MUSA: *(also suddenly frustrated)* I'm just translating!

TOM: Well what the fuck!

MUSA: It's a simple question!

TOM: What, can I *take my hand off?*

MUSA: Yes! Simple question.

TOM: I mean, I *could*. But I'm not gonna. Look would you just get out of here and let me . . .

> *Tom looks over at the girl who is for some reason sniffing his hand.*

TOM: Um, hello, excuse me.

> *The girl laughs and goes to Musa, laughing.*

GIRL: *(Arabic) His hand smells like milk.*

Reeh-et eedeh mithl il-haleeb.

ريحة ايدة مثل الحليب.

> *Musa laughs with her. As he laughs he sees something in the girl that changes him. He looks at her intently, but neither she nor Tom notices this.*

TOM: What?
(beat; Musa watches Girl) What she say!

MUSA: She says your hand smells like milk.

> *Tom smells his hand.*

TOM: It does not.

MUSA: She says it does.

TOM: *(yells at Girl, as if volume could translate)* It doesn't smell like milk!

> *The girl shrugs. Musa laughs to himself.*

MUSA: *(to Girl; Arabic) What's your name?*

Entee shismich?

انتي شاسمج؟

GIRL: *(Arabic) What's my name? What's your name? Why don't I tell everyone what your name is around here?*

Shismee? Ente shismek? Laish ma-gool ismek il kul hel-nas?

شاسمي؟ انت شاسمك؟ ليش ما اكول اسمك ال كل هلناس؟

Musa chuckles at this.

MUSA: Okay.

TOM: *What?* What are you talking about, it doesn't smell like milk.

MUSA: No, it's not that.

TOM: Then what?

MUSA: Nothing. I asked her what her name is.

TOM: Her name? I don't want to know her name, Habib.

MUSA: Okay, fine, she wouldn't tell me anyway.

TOM: What the fuck does it matter?

MUSA: *(tired of this)* It doesn't. It doesn't matter.
She just . . .
She reminds me of someone.
She reminds me of someone I knew.

TOM: Yeah? Well you remind me of *terp*, so why don't you tell her what I want and then get the fuck outta here.

GIRL: *(Arabic) I want some water. Tell him I want some water.*

Areed shwayeh muy. Gul-leh areed shwayeh muy.

اريد شوية مي. كله اريد شوية مي.

MUSA: She wants some water.

TOM: She . . . Wait, what the fuck are we even doing here? I bring her up here to do some business and . . .

GIRL: *(Arabic) I want some water.*

Areed shwayeh muy.

اريد شوية مي

TOM: Fine! Fine, water!

> *Tom goes to a bag and takes out a canteen and gives it to her.*
>
> *She sits on the bed and drinks.*
>
> *Tom watches her and smells his hand.*
>
> *He goes to Musa and sticks out his hand.*

TOM: Smell this. Does this smell like milk?

MUSA: I'm not smelling your hand, Johnny.

TOM: *Milk.* My hand doesn't smell like *milk.*

> *Tom walks to the girl. He offers his fake hand to her, which she takes. With his good hand he tenderly touches her face.*

TOM: Ficky-fick.
(*beat*) Ficky-fick with the hand.

> *Musa sits and stares at the girl.*
>
> *The girl looks at Musa. The lights shift. Tom freezes as the girl becomes Hadia, Musa's sister. Musa doesn't see her, but senses her.*

HADIA: Musa . . . Musa . . .

MUSA: Hadia . . .

HADIA: Musa, when will you take me to your garden?

MUSA: You're not my sister.

HADIA: Musa . . .

MUSA: You're not my sister.

HADIA: Of course I am . . . of course I am your sister.

MUSA: You're not . . .

You're . . .
You're not my sister.

HADIA: I want to see your garden, Musa. When will you take me to see it?

MUSA: I won't. I won't take you to see it.

HADIA: But you've told me about it. All the beautiful animals. All the green.
All that green you've told me about.

MUSA: It's not green anymore.

HADIA: Take me to see it.

MUSA: No.

HADIA: Why won't you take me?

MUSA: It's not a place for you to see.

HADIA: It sounds so beautiful.

MUSA: (*filled with regret and sadness*) Hadia, I'm . . . I'm so . . .
(*Arabic*) Hadia, I'm sorry. I'm sorry. It is my fault. Everything is my fault.

Hadia, ani mit'essif. Ani mit'essif. Hi soochi. Kul-leh soochi.

هـاديـة، انـي مـتـاسف. انـي مـتـاسف. هـاي صوجي. كـلـه صوجي.

HADIA: Tell me about it.

MUSA: You've never seen anything like it.

HADIA: Why can't I see them?

> She touches his face and he looks at her for the first time.

HADIA: Why can't I see the animals?

MUSA: Sometimes they run off.

HADIA: They're plants!

MUSA: Sometimes they fly off, to the moon.

HADIA: *(Arabic) Take me seriously!*

Ani da ahchee bjiddieh!

اني دا احجي بجدية !

MUSA: I am taking you seriously.

HADIA: Can't I come and see?
(Arabic) Musa, may I come and see your beautiful garden? Please, may I come and see it.

Musa, egder ejee ashoof hadeektek il-hilweh, reja'en, egder ejee ashoofheh

موسة، اكدر اجي اشوف حديقتك الحلوة؟ رجاء، اكدر
اجي اشوفهة

MUSA: Hadia . . . Hadia . . .
(sadly, as if defeated) Yes. Yes. You may come to my garden . . .
(he lowers his head in shame; Arabic) Hadia, I'm sorry. I'm sorry. It is my fault. Everything is my fault.

Hadia, ani mit'essif. Ani mit'essif. Hi soochi. Kul-leh soochi.

هادية، اني متاسف. هاي صوجي. كلة صوجي.

> *The lights suddenly shift back to the original scene. Tom faces upstage and the girl stands behind him, whacking him off. She has a bored look on her face. Musa snaps out of it, sees what's going on, and quickly runs out of the room.*
>
> *The girl continues. Tom yells out and hits the wall very hard three times. The girl stops and walks away from him with money in her hand. She exits. Tom leans against the wall.*
>
> *Kev enters.*

KEV: Dear Tommy,
How are you. I am fine. I am glad that you finally got some pussy. Pussy rocks. It's too bad that to get off you have to have the chick stand beside

you and yank it, but that is psychological. Don't worry. One of these days you'll figure out how to rub one off southpaw.

TOM: *(yells)* Go away!

KEV: Dear Tommy,
   How are you. I am fine.

TOM: I didn't kill you, okay? I didn't kill you. You offed yourself and I didn't have any fucking thing to do with it.

> *The garden of topiary emerges. Tiger wanders through it.*

KEV: It's not about whacking off, Tommy.
   You're not confronting the issue here.

TOM: Shut up.

KEV: You feel incomplete without your hand. You feel like you're never going to be *you* again. And so you think, "Oh, okay, I'll come back to Iraq and find my gold, and then I'll be able to whack off again." But things don't work out like that.
   Look at me. I thought I'd be in heaven by now, but I'm not. I don't know *where* I am. I'm just a reverberation of what I used to be.

TIGER: It's like God's revenge, you know? He's got us chasing our own tails here.

KEV: *(to Tiger)* I don't got a tail.
   (to Tom) Look, Tommy, I'm sorry I'm bothering you, but you're the only person who can hear me, besides the tiger, and he just keeps bugging me about epistemology and original sin, which is annoying as fuck.

TIGER: At first it's pretty cool: the limitless fruit of knowledge hanging low in your path. Then you realize it's the only thing to eat around here.

KEV: *(to Tom)* I know I annoyed you when I was alive, too. But you were cool, not like those other guys.
   You were my patron saint around here, Tommy.
   Until you were a total prick and walked out on me at the hospital.
   I needed you, you know? But you were all like, "That's your psycho problem not mine . . . "

TOM: I didn't know you were gonna kill yourself! I'm sorry, okay? I'm sorry!

TIGER: What kind of twisted bastard creates a predator and then punishes him for preying?

TOM: I wish I hadn't done that!
   But it's over now. I'm fucked up with guilt, what do you want me to do about it?

TIGER: *(examining a topiary shrub)* I have to become something else.
   I renounce tigerhood.
   I renounce myself.

KEV: We all have a psycho problem now, Tommy. Me and Tiger and you. And I'm gonna figure it out.

TIGER: If this *is* God's garden. Maybe I need to become like these plants . . . twisting and distorting my natural shape into something more pleasing to Him.

KEV: He's haunting me, and I'm haunting you . . .
   There's got to be some sort of relational algebraic equation that the three of us can factor into and solve our problem. Algebra was even *invented* here, you know? In Baghdad, by this dude, Abu Ja'far Muhammad ibn Musa al-Khwarizmi.

TOM: *How do you know this?!*

KEV: I know, right? I'm like a straight-up brainiac in the afterlife.

TIGER: You know what really bugs me? Where are the *fucking Leos*?

KEV: And algebra comes from the Arabic word *al jebr* which means "a reunion of broken parts."

TIGER: Why aren't they wandering around here, scared out of their stupid minds, contemplating their animal nature? How come it's me? How come I'm always alone every step of the way?

TOM: I'm not a bad person.

KEV: Neither was I.

TIGER: I'm a fucking saint.

KEV: It's not about being good or bad, Tommy.

TIGER: It feels like existence has become . . .

KEV: We're all just . . .

TIGER & KEV: . . . Refracted.

Tiger and Kev look at each other.

KEV: *(to Tiger)* Jinx.
Sucka!

TIGER: Fuck off.

TOM: Kev, please, leave me alone.

KEV: We're broken, man. You, me, Tiger. It's like we fell through a prism that night at the zoo and each part of ourselves just started to separate.
Does your hand still tickle? Does it still itch?
It's a phantom limb, Tommy. Just because it's gone doesn't mean it's not there.

TIGER: I'll become a plant, then. I'll cut away all the pieces of me that offend the cosmos. I'll escape my cruel nature.

Uday enters, looking at the topiary.

TIGER: But cruelty echoes all around me. Even in this ruined garden. And so I wonder if there is any escape.

Hadia enters, looking around.

MUSA: Hadia . . .

Uday approaches her, smiling. Taking her, lovingly, showing her around, showing her the topiary.

Uday puts his arm around her and leads her away.

TIGER: And I wonder if I am just an echo, repeating and repeating and repeating . . .

The lights shift back into the room with only Tom and Musa.

MUSA: She was too young for you.

TOM: What?

MUSA: The girl. She was too young for you.

TOM: What are you talking about? She was a prostitute.

MUSA: She was too young.

TOM: I gave her money.

MUSA: I'm telling you, she was too young.

TOM: It was a hand-job.

MUSA: Listen to me. Listen to me.

TOM: What?

MUSA: Listen to me.

TOM: *What?* I'm listening!

MUSA: She was . . .
Too. Young.

TOM: Fine, she was too young.
Arrest me. What the fuck are you still doing here? You like watching in on this shit?

MUSA: *You* told me to be here. *You* told me this was official military business. Official business! Ficky-fick! This is not what I signed up for.

TOM: Well, why don't you just leave then, Habib?

MUSA: *You lost your hand in battle?*
I know about your hand, Johnny.

Tom holds his hand, unconsciously self-conscious about it.

TOM: It got blown off.

MUSA: It got eaten.

TOM: How do you know that?

MUSA: Word gets around.

TOM: *How?*

Musa gets his bag.

MUSA: I knew your friend.

TOM: What friend?

MUSA: The boy who lost his mind. He said you were like his brother. He told me all about you.

Musa starts to leave.

TOM: Wait! Wait, Habib.

MUSA: What now?

TOM: You knew Kev?

MUSA: Yeah.

TOM: Did you see . . . Were you with him on that night raid?

MUSA: Yeah.

TOM: Awright, look. This is . . . I don't know if you'd know anything, but Kev . . . He had a gold gun. It was a gold-plated semiautomatic pistol. And he lost it.

MUSA: He had a gold gun.

TOM: Yeah, not that hard to remember, right?

MUSA: Yeah, I remember a gold gun.

TOM: You do.

MUSA: Not easy to forget.

TOM: Do you have it?

MUSA: Do *I* have a gold gun?

TOM: Yeah. Do you? Because it's mine.

MUSA: The military is giving away gold guns now?

TOM: No, it was personal.

MUSA: It was your *personal* gold gun.

TOM: Yeah, it was.

MUSA: You must be very rich.

TOM: I was until I lost my gun. Do you have it?

MUSA: What if I did?

TOM: *What if you did?*

MUSA: Then what?

TOM: Do you have it or not?

MUSA: I do, in fact.

TOM: Well, Jesus, I mean . . . Let me have it!

MUSA: I'm sorry . . .
  (laughs) Why would I give *you* the gun?

TOM: Why would . . . ? It's *mine*! I'm not in the mood, okay? I got a headache and I'm stressed out so just give me my gun. It's mine. I'm serious.

MUSA: No, you're not serious.

TOM: I'm not? You want to test me?

MUSA: You don't know what is serious.
  You have no investment in this gun, it does not mean anything to you outside of the fact that it is gold. You're looting so you have something, something to take home. I don't care about what you have to take home, Johnny.

TOM: What the fuck are you talking about?

MUSA: What the fuck? What the fuck are *you* talking about, Johnny?

TOM: My name's not Johnny!

MUSA: My name's not Habib.

TOM: What's your problem, man?

MUSA: You don't listen.

TOM: You *work* for us! I could have you fired, how would you like that?

MUSA: And what would you say anyhow? That I stole your gold gun pilfered from the Hussein brothers' stash? There are rules for you. For me, there are not rules. No rules, nothing. Anarchy, yes. Rules? No. So go fuck yourself, Johnny. My English is getting better every day. Maybe I go get a job at CNN.

TOM: You know what happens if they find a firearm on your person?

MUSA: How stupid do you think I am? That I'm going to just give it back?
      We will work out a deal. You get me some things, I give you the gold gun.

TOM: Jesus. What do you want?

MUSA: Do we have a deal?

TOM: What do you *want*? I'm not going to make a deal unless I know what you want.

MUSA: But you're willing to negotiate?

TOM: I'm willing to kick your fucking head in, Habib. What the fuck do you want?

> *Beat.*

MUSA: I want weapons.

TOM: You want weapons.

MUSA: Guns, ammunition, and hand grenades.
      And then I will give you the gold gun.

TOM: Oh, yeah, okay. Because I'm an *arms dealer*, Habib. I'll get you a bunch of fucking weapons. Who do you think I am?

MUSA: You are a marine and you are a thief.

TOM: Yeah, and I get you weapons. Then what? Next thing I know, you're blowing us all away?
   What am I, a jerk? You think I'm just going to supply some crazy terrorist with guns and shit?

MUSA: I'm not a terrorist.

TOM: Yeah, then what are you?

MUSA: I'm a gardener.

TOM: Don't get metaphorical with me, prick. You're all the fucking same.

MUSA: No! No, you don't listen!

TOM: *What?*

MUSA: I'm a *gardener*! Do you understand? I'm not a terrorist! I'm not an arms dealer! I'm not a translator or "terp."
   I am a gardener!

TOM: Fine! So you're a gardener! So what!?

MUSA: You don't understand . . . you don't understand . . .

TOM: What don't I understand?

MUSA: I am an artist! I am an artist!

TOM: Yeah, okay, you're an artist.
   Gold gun. Where is it?

MUSA: And weapons?

TOM: I'm not getting you a bunch of fucking weapons, okay!?

MUSA: Then you're not getting the gold gun! This is not complicated! Capitalism! Thank you! Now you want something for nothing?

TOM: What do you want with a bunch of weapons anyway?

MUSA: What do you think I have to my name? A stupid job with U.S. Military? And what about when you all leave? What will I have then?
   I'll have a bunch of guns and bullets I can sell because that will be the only thing worth anything. Is that so crazy?

TOM: Yeah, it's crazy.

MUSA: I am tired, do you understand?!
I am tired of making the same mistake *over and over and over again.*
I always work for the wrong people.
I always serve the tyrants.
Not anymore.
I am tired of being made a fool.

> *Tom walks away from Musa, rubbing his eyes,*
> *exhausted.*

MUSA: It's a simple deal.
What you want and what I want.
Isn't this how the world is supposed to work?

> *A long beat between them.*

TOM: *(not looking at him; still rubbing his eyes)* She wasn't that young.

MUSA: Do we have a deal?

Scene 2.

> *A bombed-out building, half-standing, in the middle*
> *of the desert, south of Baghdad. The middle of the*
> *night. The place is ghostly, ethereal, haunted. Kev*
> *appears, as if he's been wandering in the desert.*
>
> *Kev speaks in Arabic.*

KEV: *(Arabic) I am lost in the desert.*

Anee tayeh bil sahra'.

اني تايه بالصحراء.

God, I am lost in the desert and I am calling out to you in prayer. Because
I have never before prayed, I am praying to you in a different language
because the very strangeness of it makes me feel like perhaps you would
understand.

Ulleh, anee tayeh bil sahra' oo da ed'eelek, anee b'oomree me di'ait gebul, bess hisse da ed'eelek bgair lugeh. A'roof hathe shee ghereeb bess emelee inoo tigder tiftehimnee.

الله، انـي تـايـه بـالـصحراء و دا ادعيلك. انـي بـعـمري مـا دعيت كـبل، بـس دادعيلك هسة بـغير لـغة، اعرف هـاذة شي غـريـب بـس املـي انـو تـكدر تـفـتـهمني.

(he holds his severed hand high above his head, as if to offer it to God)
Take my hand, heal my severed body, take me from the desert. Let my mind find peace.

Ukhuth eedee, ishfee gissmee ilmitgetta', ikhithnee min il-sahraa'. Khelee bal-ee yirtahh.

اخـذ ايـدي، اشفـي جسمـي المكطع، اخـدنـي مـن الـصحراء. خلـي بـالي يـرتـاح.

> A beat. Kev realizes nothing is happening and lowers his hand, looks at it, and then looks skyward, a little defeated now.

KEV: *(English)* Or not.
Maybe I should say a Hail Mary?
I know how it works, Man. You're not gonna come down and explain everything to me.
But I figure You're out *there, somewhere.*
I never expected to know so much. I never knew there was so much to know. And the very fact that I'm *around*? The very fact that I'm *learning* all these things? I gotta figure there's something going on a little more important than just haunting Tommy.
So what happens now, God? What happens now that I'm intelligent and aware and sensitive to the universe?

TIGER: I'll tell you what happens: God leans down just close enough and whispers into your ear: *Go fuck yourself.*
And then He's gone.

> Tiger holds some small, indistinguishable bloody carcass, his face is covered in blood.

KEV: Thought you gave up killing animals.

TIGER: I was hungry. Sue me. What's He gonna do? Punish me more? I dare Him. I dare Him to come down and tell me what a bad tiger I am.
  Look, I tried. For a good two to three hours I was a vegetarian. But guess what? Vegetables taste like shit.
  We're just stuck here, son. Mastodons in the tar pit of life-after-death. And I'm tired, and I'm not a saint, I'm just the biggest predatory cat in the entire fucking world. So I'm gonna kill something, and I'm gonna eat it and I'm gonna wave this bloody carcass in God's face and tell him, *You knew I was a tiger when You made me, motherfucker.*

KEV: I wasn't talking to you.

TIGER: Ha. You were praying, huh?
  Well, you raise your voice and I'm the only one who hears it.
  What if *I'm* God. Did you ever think about that?

KEV: God ain't a tiger.

TIGER: Maybe He is. Maybe I'm Him. Maybe Him's Me.

KEV: Prove it.

TIGER: Go fuck yourself.

KEV: Can You give me one little sign to let me know that my voice is being heard by You? Then *I* can haunt *You* through prayer! *I* could haunt *You*, God!
  (beat) Your friend, Kev.

Scene 3.

> The same place, the bombed-out building, half-standing, in the middle of the desert, south of Baghdad. However, there is daylight, the place is less ghostly.
>
> Musa enters, hot, dusty. The sound of a jeep idling, and then the sound stops.
>
> Tom enters.

MUSA: This is wrong. *This is wrong!*

TOM: Would you shut up!

MUSA: We need to leave!

TOM: I said we'd be fine.

MUSA: *Fine?* This is the middle of the desert! If the sun goes down, we won't find our way back to the road!

TOM: Would you relax? This is it.

MUSA: This is what? There's nothing here.

TOM: It got bombed.

MUSA: So where are the guns?

TOM: Just wait, okay? Just calm down.

MUSA: You brought me all the way out to the middle of nowhere? Where are the weapons?

TOM: Don't get pushy, Habib. Relax.

MUSA: No weapons? Then we have to leave. Right now.

> *Tom gets in Musa's face.*

TOM: We're not leaving until I say we leave.

> *A strange woman in a tattered black shroud hobbles on to the stage. Her face cannot be seen. She has stumps for hands.*
>
> *Tom and Musa see her. They both step back and shudder, but Tom knows who she is.*

TOM: *(to Woman)*

El-salamu-aleikum.

السلام علیكم.

WOMAN: U-aleikum el-Salaam.

و علیكم السلام.

MUSA: What's happened to her?

TOM: She's a leper.
There were a bunch of them living here.
It was a leper colony.
Habib, ask her what happened.

> *Musa looks at Tom, at the woman, back at the jeep.*
> *He sighs.*

MUSA: *(Arabic) What happened here?*

Hi sh-sar ihna?

هـاي شمـار ا هنـا؟

WOMAN: *(Arabic) A bomb.*

Kumbuleh.

قـنـبـلـة .

MUSA: A bomb.

TOM: Yeah, we know that. Where are the others? Where are her . . .
you know, her fellow lepers.

MUSA: *(Arabic) Where are the others who live here?*

Weyn bukeeyet il-nas il-sakneen ihna?

ويـن بـقـيـة الـنـاس الـسـاكـنـين ا هنـا؟

WOMAN: *(Arabic) They died.*

Matou.

مـاتـو .

MUSA: They died.

TOM: She's all alone?

MUSA: Yes.

TOM: Ask her where my bag is.

MUSA: Your bag?

TOM: Yeah.

Musa starts to translate but then stops.

MUSA: *(to Tom)* What type of bag?

TOM: What do you mean.

MUSA: You said bag.

TOM: Yeah, my bag! Ask her where it is.

MUSA: What kind! Big bag? Little bag? Luggage?

TOM: A bag! A fucking bag! Just fucking translate!

MUSA: There are different words for different bags!

TOM: Just *translate*!

MUSA: *(frustrated; Arabic) This man says he left a bag here. Do you know where his bag is?*

Hathe el-rijal yigool tirrek chees ihna, tu'ruffeen weyn cheesseh?

هاذة الرجال يكول ترك جيس، اهنا تعرفين وين جيسه؟

WOMAN: *(Arabic) What bag?*

Ya chees?

يا جيس؟

MUSA: What bag?

TOM: I left a bag here, and I told them I was coming back and they told me they'd keep it and now I'm back and I'm not coming back again! Ask her where the fucking bag is Habib, or we're going to have a problem!

WOMAN: *(Arabic, calmly) There is no bag. There is nothing here.*

Makoo ay chees. Makoo shee ihna.

ماكو اي جيس. ماكو شي اهنا.

TOM: *(to Musa)* What she say?

MUSA: She doesn't know a bag.
The whole place has been destroyed. She's living in the rubble.

She doesn't have anything.
She doesn't have your bag.

WOMAN: *(Arabic) Do you want some water?*

Treed shwayeh muy?

تـريـد شـويـة مـي؟

TOM: What now?

MUSA: She wants to know if you want some water.

TOM: *(losing his shit) I want my fucking toilet seat!*

> The woman goes back into the ruin.

TOM: What . . . where's she . . . Where are you going?! Hey!

> Tom rushes to the ruin and peers in after her.

TOM: What the fuck man, this is making me nuts, I swear to God . . .

MUSA: We need to leave. The sun is going down.

TOM: We can leave when I get my toilet seat.

MUSA: What toilet seat!? We came here for my weapons.

TOM: Habib, seriously? You really think I brought you out here to get weapons? I needed a terp. I need to get my toilet seat.

MUSA: So where are the weapons?

TOM: *There are no weapons! Wake up!*

MUSA: You lied to me . . .

TOM: Hey, call her. Tell her to come back.

MUSA: You lied to me!

TOM: So what?

MUSA: We came here for a *toilet seat?*
Do you hear how you talk?! Listen! Toilet seat! Toilet seat! You want something to shit on!

TOM: It's a *gold* toilet seat.

Musa takes this information in.

MUSA: Gold. Gold toilet seat . . . Gold toilet seat . . .

TOM: Make sense now?

MUSA: I follow you around like a dog, everywhere. Ficky-fick, ficky-fick, the middle of the desert, so you can have sex, so you can get a toilet seat so you can shit all over this place.

TOM: It's a job, Habib. Do your job.

MUSA: *(takes out the gold gun)* Yeah, Johnny . . . a job.
A job.

TOM: Check it out man . . . you actually brought it with you. Holy shit.

MUSA: Yes, check me out.

TOM: Give it to me, Habib.

MUSA: You want the gun, Johnny?

TOM: Give me the fucking gun.

MUSA: *(points it at Tom)* You want the gun, but you lie to me.
You want the gun, I want to leave.

TOM: *Don't you point that at me!*

MUSA: *(stops pointing) Or what?! What will you do now? What else can you do to me now?!*

TOM: I said we can leave when I get my—

Musa shoots Tom in the stomach.

MUSA: Your toilet seat! Yes! You need a toilet seat! And you need your gold gun! You need gold gold gold and fuck you and your gold and your goddamn bullshit all the time!

TOM: *You shot me . . .*
You fucking shot me . . .

*Musa points the gun at Tom as if to shoot him
again.*

MUSA: *(his rage giving way to tears)* I am tired! I am so tired of
everyone . . .

TOM: Stop it . . . Stop it, please God, stop it . . .

> *Musa stands over Tom and puts the gun to Tom's
> head.*

MUSA: Don't pray to God. Don't you pray to any god, you piece of shit,
man. No god is going to hear you. Not out here. Not anymore . . . no
god is going to . . . no god is . . .

> *Musa takes the gun away. He stares at Tom.*

TOM: I'm sorry . . . I'm sorry . . . Please . . .

> *Musa exits, quickly.*

> *Tom crawls and props himself up on a rock.*

TOM: Habib . . . ! Habib, don't leave me here . . . I mean . . . I'm
sorry . . .

(he coughs; he winces in pain)

> *The leper enters.*

WOMAN: *(Arabic)* Do you want water?

Treed muy?

تـريـد مـي؟

> *Tom is startled by her voice.*

TOM: Who's there? Who said that?

WOMAN: *(Arabic)* Do you want water?

Treed muy?

تـريـد مـي؟

TOM: I'm hurt.

WOMAN: *(Arabic) Do you want water?*

Treed muy?

تـريـد مـي؟

TOM: I don't know what you're saying.
I don't understand.

> *Kev enters from the ruins, carrying a duffel bag.*
> *Both Tom and the woman turn and look at him.*

TOM: Oh God, here we go . . .

KEV: El-salamu-aleikum.

الـسلام عـليـكم.

WOMAN: U-aleikum el-Salaam.

و عـليـكم الـسلام.

TOM: Kev . . . Kev . . . You gotta help me, man . . .

> *Kev takes a gold toilet seat from the bag.*

KEV: Hey Tommy. This yours?

TOM: Kev, can you help me? Can you go get help for me? I got shot, man!

WOMAN: *(Arabic) Does he want water?*

Yireed muy?

يـريـد مـي؟

KEV: *(to Tom)* She wants to know if you want some water.

TOM: Can you go get help?

KEV: From who?

TOM: *Anyone! Anyone,* okay!?

KEV: I can get you some water. How about that?

TOM: She has water?

KEV: I guess so.

TOM: Wait . . . You speak Arabic?

KEV: I kind of picked it up in death.

TOM: Well, how come she can see you too?

KEV: Dude, I don't know all the fucking rules okay?

TOM: Jesus. Yes! Yes, I want some water!

> *The woman hobbles into the ruins.*

KEV: What's it like getting shot?

TOM: It sucks.

KEV: Yeah.

TOM: Can't you go tell someone I'm here? Please Kev, can't you do that?

KEV: Sorry, man. But this is the best I can do.

> *The woman hobbles out from the ruins with a
> goatskin flask slung around her shoulders. She
> brings it to Tom and drops it in his lap.*

TOM: Thank you.

> *Tom drinks.*

TOM: Oh . . . man . . . *Okay.* I gotta get back to the jeep . . .

KEV: Habib took the jeep.

TOM: Aw fuck! Okay, come on . . .
What else . . .
Look can you ask her if she knows anyone around here? I'm dying,
Kev, can you ask her if she can help me?

KEV: (*Arabic*) *My friend is dying. Can you help him out?*

Sedeekee day-moot. Tigdereen itsa'dee?

صديقي دي موت. تكدرين تساعدي؟

WOMAN: (*Arabic*) *I have a first-aid kit.*

Endee isa'fat aweliye.

عندي اسعافات اولية

KEV: She said she has a first-aid kit.

TOM: She has first-aid!? She's a *leper*, she's got a first-aid kit!?

KEV: That's what she said.

TOM: Fuck, man! Tell her to go get it!

> *Kev nods at the woman, she reenters the ruins.*

TOM: I'm not gonna die here . . . I'm not gonna die. I'm gonna fuckin fight through this, you know?

KEV: At least you got your toilet seat.

TOM: (*clutching toilet seat closer*) Fuck you.

> *The woman enters with a very old metal box. She gives it to Kev.*

TOM: Oh, God, thank you . . . thank you so much . . . thank you . . .

> *Kev opens the box, and turns it upside down. A Band-Aid floats out of it.*

TOM: (*directed at no one; half-laughing, half-crying*) *I got shot in the stomach what the fuck I need with a Band-Aid!*

> *He coughs, clutches his stomach. Realizes he's dying for sure.*

TOM: Oh, God . . .

Kev, I'm gonna die.

KEV: Yeah, man, I know.

TOM: No . . . no no no . . .
I can't believe I'm going to die.
I can't believe I'm going to die *here*. Out here in the middle of
nowhere.
I'm from Michigan.
It's shaped like a mitten.
I was never supposed to die here.
(beat) What happens when you die?

KEV: You know when you've been drinking all night? And you start
to fade? And you can't keep your eyes open, even when you're talking?
That's how it goes, man. It's not too bad.

TOM: I don't want to die.

KEV: Yeah, I know.

TOM: Tell her . . . tell her I don't want to die.

KEV: *(Arabic) He doesn't want to die.*

Hoo-eh mayreed ymoot.

هـوة مـريـد يـمـوت.

WOMAN: *(Arabic) My body has been decaying for my whole life.*

Jissmi de-yit'akel ttul hayati.

جسمي ديـتـاكـل طول حيـاتـي.

TOM: What . . . what she say?

KEV: She said that she has been decaying her whole life.

WOMAN: *(Arabic) I am made of sand.*

Ani masnoo'a min remmull.

انـي مـصنـوعة مـن رمـل.

KEV: She says she is made of sand.

TOM: She's made of sand.

KEV: Yeah.

TOM: Can you ask her how long she's not had any hands?
How long she's just had stumps.

> Kev thinks. He then asks the woman in Arabic.

KEV: (Arabic) He would like to know how long you have not had your hands.

Yireed yu'roof shked sar-lich bidoon eedain.

يـريـد يـعرف شكد صارلج بـدون ايـديـن.

WOMAN: (Arabic) When I was fourteen years old they fell off. They slowly fell off over time.

Min chan oumri arbata'ash seneh eedainatee wig'ow. Wig'ow shwaya, shwaya bmuroor il-ayam.

مـن جـان عـمـري اربـاطعش سنة ايـديـنـاتـي وكـعـو. وكـعـو
شـويـة شـويـة بمرور الايـام.

KEV: Since she was fourteen.
She said they slowly just fell off.

> Tom shows his hand to the woman.

TOM: (to Woman) This is what you get now if you lose your hand.
It's top of the line.
It smells like milk.

TOM: Don't leave me, Kev.

> The woman speaks to him plainly.

WOMAN: (Arabic) Nothing.

Wala-shee.

ولا شـي.

There is no God.

Makoo Ulleh.

ماكوا الله

No heaven, no hell.

La jenna, wala je-hen-nem.

لا جنـة و لا جهـنم.

Death is nothing. It is peaceful.

Il-moat moo-shee. Il-moat musalim.

الموت هـو شي. الموت مسالم.

Scene 4.

> *The garden of topiary. Musa enters. He walks to a topiary shrub.*

MUSA: *(hushed, whispered, to himself)* My horse. My poor horse.
(goes to another topiary) Look at you . . . Such a pretty . . . so lovely . . .

> *Uday enters.*

UDAY: Oh, Mansour!
Uday is so *proud!*
Stupid Kid American. Ha!
He suffered, Mansour. He died slowly in the desert all alone.
And do you know what the best thing? He called out for you!
Begging you to come back and save him!
He *begged* you! Ha!
Fuck me, man, you're good! That's advanced: getting a man to beg you to come back to him *after* you've shot him!? And shot him why? Because he was *annoying* you! Because he wouldn't shut up.
I agree. Annoying people should all be shot and left to die. Because fuck them!
Mansour. Oh, Mansour.
Uday is so proud.

MUSA: You don't know anything. It wasn't supposed to happen. I didn't want to kill him.

UDAY: I know what you mean. Accidents like that are happening to Uday all the time.

MUSA: I'm not like you are . . .
I am not the kind of person who does this. It is not who I am.

UDAY: Sometimes we *change*. As people. This is the type of shit they teach you in boarding school.
Like you: how one day you are translating, and another day you are shooting people because they annoy you.

MUSA: *That's not why I killed him!*

UDAY: *(excited)* Then why?

MUSA: Not because of that.

UDAY: You tell me. Tell me why. Uday wants to know. *Why?*

MUSA: Because . . . we were in the desert . . .
and the sun was going down . . .
And . . .
(beat) And the sun was going down.

UDAY: . . . What?

MUSA: *(quiet)* The sun was going down.

UDAY: *The sun was going down!*
(claps with delight) Holy shit my man, that's your excuse!? The sun?!
That's all it takes, eh Mansour? You know that happens *every day*, right? The sun *goes down*. Fuck me, even my *father* needed better reasons than that!
I thought you were good, Mansour, but this?

Musa holds the gun out.

MUSA: Take it back.

UDAY: It's yours now. You've earned it.

MUSA: I'll never use it again.

UDAY: Come on! Not even once?

MUSA: Never.

UDAY: Don't tell me you didn't like it! It felt a little bit good, didn't it? Killing the boy, leaving him to die.

When you realized the bullet hit, that it caused pain, you felt *relief*. I know it, man. The pain *went away*.

MUSA: Yes, the pain went away.

UDAY: Good. You're beginning to learn about survival.

MUSA: It brought him to his knees.

UDAY: Yeah, yeah, and then?

MUSA: He screamed. He prayed to God.

UDAY: And you told him . . . ?

MUSA: I told him not to pray to God. I told him no god would ever hear him.

UDAY: Nice. Good line.

MUSA: I stood above him and pressed the gun to his head.

UDAY: But you let him live. Better he can suffer.

MUSA: No. No more, no more . . .

> *Musa puts the gun in Uday's hand.*

UDAY: Mansour . . . you can't let go now! You have a taste for blood. You like it. You want it again and again and again.

> *Uday holds out the gun. Musa spits on it.*

UDAY: This is very rude, Mansour. Very rude.

You know what your problem is Mansour?

MUSA: I don't have a problem.

UDAY: Your problem is this: the best thing you've ever done, in your entire life, was only possible because of me. Without Uday, you're just a petty gardener.

> *Uday goes to the gun, picks it up, wipes it on his coat.*

UDAY: *With* Uday, on another hand, you're the artist, building topiary, doing these great things. Because *I* wanted them. Because *I* employed you. Because *I* provided you with thousands of gallons of water in the middle of the fucking desert.

MUSA: This is *my* garden.

UDAY: No, Mister Fuck-Shit! This is *Uday's* garden! You think this place is *yours*? These animals are *yours*? Even your *memory*? It all belongs to Uday.

MUSA: No, no, I can remember a life without you . . . I can remember my sister without you . . .

UDAY: *(beat; Uday leans in to Musa)* When the blades of your shears touched her skin, she burst like a grape.
    Ruined my suit.

> *Uday holds the gun out.*

UDAY: Oh Hadia. Hadia Hadia Hadia. Such a small creature, making such a great noise.

> *Musa stares at him and then takes the gun.*

UDAY: Good boy. You take it, and go out tomorrow, and find someone else. It will be easy. The sun will set and you'll have no choice but to kill somebody.

> *Musa points the gun to his own head.*

UDAY: *(exasperated)* No, Mansour . . . Someone *else*.

MUSA: I won't be like you. I am myself. I am myself.

> *Hadia enters, slowly strolling through the topiary, looking at it, spellbound. Covering her eyes.*

HADIA: Can I look yet? Can I look now, Musa?

MUSA: Not yet.

UDAY: Don't you bring her into this, Mansour! I will take her again.

HADIA: I want to see it! Let me see the garden, Musa! Can I look?

UDAY: I will do it all again. I will tear her to pieces again and again and again . . .

Musa leaves Uday and goes to her.

MUSA: You can look but then you have to go. But for now, Hadia . . . Open your eyes.

HADIA: A lion! A camel . . . an elephant . . . a . . . What is that?

MUSA: That is my giraffe.

HADIA: How do you do it?

MUSA: I don't know. It's difficult to explain.

UDAY: Fine, okay . . .
(*starts to move toward Hadia*) This is not going to end well, boss.

HADIA: It's beautiful here.

MUSA: It is.

HADIA: Who could have ever thought, eh Musa? That such a place could be here? That trees could grow like this? Who could have ever thought?

MUSA: Hadia . . . leave now. Go home. Go home quickly. Never come back. Leave.

HADIA: I'll leave in a moment. I want to see the rest.

Uday takes Hadia by the arm, holding her firmly.

UDAY: You could stay in this garden forever, man. Watching me and her, me and her, me and her . . .
Is this what you want to see?
Okay, man. Watch. I'm going to take her back there and make her into a topiary. This time, I'm going to wear a bib.
Oh, one more thing . . .

That boy you killed . . .
He was the boy who killed me.
Thank you, Mansour.
Thank you.
Thank you.
Thank you.

> *Uday exits with Hadia.*

MUSA: *(to Uday, but to himself)* I will live with your voice, okay?
I will live with it.
It doesn't matter, because my hands belong to me.
And my hands have their own memory.
And when I put them on a plant, they create something.
They will *create* something.

> *Musa says it but he has not convinced himself.*
>
> *He cocks the gun and stares at it.*
>
> *Tiger approaches and stands behind Musa. Musa doesn't see Tiger.*

TIGER: Look, I don't mean to interrupt, but I couldn't help overhearing . . .
Did you make this place?

> *Musa looks at Tiger. Takes in the reality of a ghost of a tiger before him, seems to be okay with it.*

MUSA: I made this place.

TIGER: Are You who I think You are?

MUSA: I don't know who I am.

TIGER: Look, I've been looking for You, I've been calling out Your name.

MUSA: *(covers his eyes in exhaustion)*
Too many ghosts. Ghosts everywhere.

TIGER: It's not just me! I brought this girl here. She'd been killed, you know? She was just a little girl. She wanted to know when You'd be back. She wanted to know how You made these things. All these animals. Elephant, horse, giraffe . . .

MUSA: This garden is a wound. I want this place to burn, I want to set it on fire.

TIGER: Wait! I mean . . . The girl . . . She's not going to like that very much.

MUSA: *(turns to Tiger)* Tell her I'm sorry. Tell her I'm not who she thought I was. Tell her I've done horrible things, and I . . .
I don't know what I'm going to do next.
Tell her to forget about me.
I've become a different man.

> *Musa puts the gun in his pants.*

TIGER: You're not a man. You're God.

MUSA: No. I am not.

> *Musa starts to leave.*

TIGER: Yes, You are! I've been waiting for You. I've been waiting for You to speak.

MUSA: God has spoken. This world. This is what He's said.

> *Musa exits.*

TIGER: *This?*
This isn't enough!
I want You to say more than this.
You know what? You belong in a cage.
We should hunt You down lock You up just like every other wild thing in the world.
I can see it: God in a cage, right here. Finally get a look at You.
All the great mysteries of creation could be revealed at the zoo.
Come see the God exhibit! Come watch the beast play!

And we, the lousy dead, innumerable and in constant parade, would finally have our Holy Land . . . a cage in a garden in a burning city. Ohhh . . . What a fucking sight!

> *His eyes shut in a dream, a fantasy, for a moment. Then he opens them and realizes he is alone.*

I'm fuckin hungry.

> *He goes to get the first-aid kit. Comes back, puts it down.*

So I'm just gonna sit back and wait for something to walk by so I can kill it and eat it.
Rules of the hunt . . .
Don't fuckin move. Don't make a sound.
Be conscious of the wind: where's it coming from.
Be still.
Watch.
Listen.

ACKNOWLEDGMENTS

RAJIV JOSEPH would like to thank: the Lark Play Development Center program, through which all three of these plays were developed; SUNY Purchase School of the Arts Conservatory of Theatre Arts and Film; Second Stage Theatre; the Center Theatre Group; the Alley Theatre; the National Endowment for the Arts; Giovanna Sardelli; Vanessa Gould; OrigamiUSA; and the Narcissist Book Club.